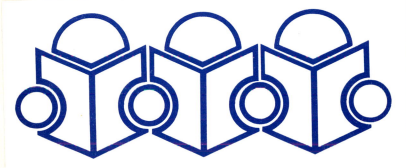

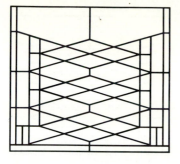

THE NATURE OF FRANK LLOYD WRIGHT

THE NATURE OF
FRANK LLOYD WRIGHT

EDITED BY CAROL R. BOLON, ROBERT S. NELSON, AND LINDA SEIDEL

THE UNIVERSITY OF CHICAGO PRESS   CHICAGO AND LONDON

CAROL R. BOLON is assistant professor
in the departments of Art and South Asian
Languages and Civilizations at the University
of Chicago. ROBERT S. NELSON is
associate professor in the Department of Art at
the University of Chicago. LINDA SEIDEL is
associate professor in the Department of Art at
the University of Chicago and the author of
*Songs of Glory: The Romanesque Facades of
Aquitaine,* also published by the University of
Chicago Press.

The University of Chicago Press, Chicago 60637
The University of Chicago Press, Ltd., London
© 1988 by The University of Chicago
All rights reserved. Published 1988
Printed in the United States of America
97 96 95 94 93 92 91 90 89 88   5 4 3 2

Library of Congress Cataloging in Publication Data

The Nature of Frank Lloyd Wright.

    Papers presented at a symposium; organized, to
celebrate the 75th anniversary of Frank Lloyd Wright's
Robie House, by the Dept. of Art of the University of
Chicago, and held Oct. 1984.
    Includes index.
    1. Wright, Frank Lloyd, 1867–1959—Criticism
and interpretation—Congresses.   2. Architecture,
Modern—20th century—United States—Congresses.
I. Bolon, Carol R.   II. Nelson, Robert S.,
1947–   .   III. Seidel, Linda.   IV. University
of Chicago. Dept. of Art.
NA737.W7N38   1988   720'.92'4   87-13764
ISBN 0-226-06351-8

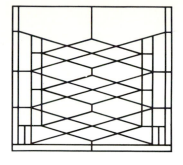

CONTENTS

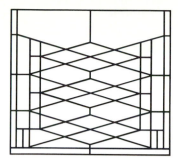

ILLUSTRATIONS

CONTENTS

CONTENTS

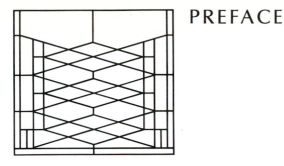

PREFACE

In October 1984 the Department of Art of the University of Chicago organized a symposium in celebration of the seventy-fifth anniversary of Frank Lloyd Wright's Robie house, a landmark building on the university's campus. Eight of the papers that were presented on that occasion have been revised and are published here; each of these offers fresh insight into Wright's achievement, particularly the relation of his professional practice and personal philosophy to nature. Taken together, these papers provide a provocative interpretation of Wright's originality and present a reevaluation of his work in relation to that of his predecessors and his contemporaries, architects as well as writers.

The conference for which these papers were originally prepared was supported by the Illinois Arts Council, both the College and the Women's Board of the University of Chicago, and Thomas Eyerman of Skidmore, Owings, and Merrill. We are grateful to the individuals involved for their generosity in helping us realize that goal. Kim Clawson of the Society of Architectural Historians (Chicago chapter), John Zukowsky of the Art Institute of Chicago, Timothy Rub of the Cooper-Hewitt Museum, and conference participants Neil Levine and David van Zanten all offered invaluable advice during the planning of the symposium. We acknowledge, with appreciation, their kind assistance during that critical phase. Finally, we are indebted to friends and colleagues on campus for their aid during the conference and throughout the preparation of this volume. Mary Bartholomew, Richard Born, Neil Harris, Reinhold Heller, Jonathan Kleinbard, Mary Kong, Donald N. Levine, Peter Sampson, and Stuart M. Tave all made special efforts in our behalf at different times. This project, from inception to completion, could not have succeeded so well without them.

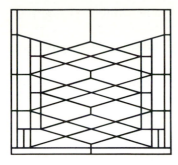

INTRODUCTION

VINCENT SCULLY

The Robie house rises, heavy as a mountain, buoyant as an airplane. Its interior spaces are caverns deep in the ground, platforms in the air. We find the doorway with some difficulty, enter into constriction and darkness, and are carried forward and upward to the light, looming like Titans under ceilings barely high enough to contain us and over fireplaces scaled around our knees. Everything gives away around us, leading our eyes to infinite distances. We are at the heart of a mystery: giants, children, and free.

Wright's work is close to us and far away. History's gulf has opened between us. The marked resurgence of scholarship now directed toward Wright derives in part from a tacit recognition of that fact. Wright has become a historical figure. He lived in an age different from our own: near but different in fundamental ways that are still difficult to pinpoint or understand. Nor has Wright left any direct descendants to help bridge the gap. The Taliesin Fellowship has not provided a successor to him or even a body of work worthy of association with his name. There are surely many reasons for this sad fact. One of them was the dominance of Mrs. Wright over the Fellowship in the long years between Wright's death in 1959 and her own in 1985. "Mr. Wright was a great architect," one of the later apprentices said to me in 1978, "but Mrs. Wright has a better sense of color." This was at a time when the Fellowship was perverting the restoration of such key monuments as Unity Temple with garish Amerindian color schemes of Mrs. Wright's choosing, totally at odds with the gentle, silver tonalities Wright had actually used and which archaeology had painstakingly brought to light.

Another reason for the artistic bankruptcy of the Fellowship goes more deeply back to Wright's own time at its head. He set himself up as the only model, stunting the capacity of his apprentices to grow in architectural culture and to construct individual models of their own. His own career clearly shows something he tended to conceal from them: that his work represented what Freud would have called a continual "condensation" of multiple sources into "new unities" with a special richness of their own. He himself had many models and used the work of numerous contemporary architects and past cultures to get himself going, but he denied his apprentices access to that essential process.

Wright himself is so complex—and was great precisely because of it—that he richly rewards many different kinds of study. Larzer Ziff's literary analogies, for example, are more than welcome, and Julia Meech-Pekarik's admirably tough-minded paper on Wright as a collector and dealer in Japanese prints is still another way into these mysteries. It illuminates Wright's trenchant, hard, and realistic side, what he called the "merchant" in himself. An appreciation of that iron figures in very few analyses of him, but it was an essential part of his character, and it permitted him to face some very difficult times in his life and to get on with his work. Japanese woodcuts were also one of his sources of inspiration which, as Meech-Pekarik points out, he did not conceal from his apprentices but brought actively to their attention, using them for teaching in the drafting room.

Contextual studies of Wright in his society are also a major need at this time, and Gwendolyn Wright's is a serious example of the genre. It is salutary to find Wright's views on society as a whole and planning in particular explored in this fashion, but in the end it is amazing to observe how comparatively little more such studies seem able to tell us about his essential way of designing. And it is always in that area that we most want to know more about him—that area of artistic creation where, with each passing year, he seems ever more unique. Earlier studies of the work of his colleagues of the Prairie school, such as those by H. Allen Brooks and Mark L. Peisch, from which a great deal was once hoped in terms of "putting Wright in his place," have had the opposite effect. The more we know of the others the more special he seems. It is his presence, his mystery, that looms larger all the time.

From that point of view, David Van Zanten's paper seems especially timely, since it tries both to explore Wright's method of design and to situate it in a group effort of architects in Chicago around 1900. It makes fascinating reading; Wright's "unit" system is more clearly described here than ever before. Sullivan's participation in the general professional movement was new to me, touching in a personal way and heartening from the point of view of professional brotherhood and cooperation. But in the end the group dissolves. Its attempt to achieve "total design" comes to nothing; only Wright remains, somehow going on to new stages of growth while the energies of his contemporaries are draining away. Again, why is this? Here Wright's Froebel connections should not be dismissed so easily as Van Zanten seems to dismiss them, for not only does Wright give them prominence in his own account of his design, but also, and perhaps more to the point, they clearly reveal themselves in the forms of his buildings. Those stripped, blocky masses were all unmistakably Froebelian long before Wright had a unit system, and they retained that character right through the period when the unit system achieved mature form—that system itself suggested in good part by Froebel. Most of all, what the abstractions of Froebel seem to have given Wright—along with the "conventionalized" motifs after nature he found in Owen Jones—was a kind of fundamental design energy, a confidence that in this way he was truly constructing the world, not, as he said, "representing" it. Here of course we are led to the most cohesive body of papers in this collection, those by Beeby, Connors, Hoffman, and Levine, all of which deal in one way or another with the theme of Wright and Nature.

This is not a simple topic. It is true that, as a nineteenth-century Romantic, Wright duly ascribed all virtues to Nature and credited her with acting at least as the inspiration for his own work, sometimes perhaps as its objective. In this he was a faithful disciple of Ruskin, whom he read in youth. But it was Owen Jones he traced, and, as Catherine Lynn has shown elsewhere, Ruskin unconditionally condemned "conventionalizations" of Jones's type as wholly unnatural, destructive to Art and, indeed, to society as a whole, leading it irremediably toward

"Hindoo depravity." So there is a kind of paradox right at the beginning of Wright's work, one intensified by the abstractions of Froebel, and Joseph Connors attempts to explore it in his paper, *Wright on Nature and the Machine*. Yet, while he by no means ignores the evidence provided by Wright's work itself, Connors still bases his argument on a straight reading of Wright's words, and here Wright can be very tricky indeed. One of his many wonderful sides was that of the American confidence man, the bunko artist with a fast line of patter. He was so intelligent, so quick, and so ruthlessly directed toward getting his buildings built that he was often capable of saying quite contradictory things to create the effect he desired. (Philip Johnson resembles him in this, if at some distance.) So Wright's words cannot invariably be trusted or taken at face value. They must sometimes be read with some irony. The trick, I suppose, is to know when not to do so. At the same time, verbal homage to Nature is so built into Wright's cultural structure that it can deflect us, unless we are wary, from recognizing the obvious, abstract systems that in fact shaped his design, as in Froebel's blocks and Van Zanten's unit. Connors is well aware of this, so proposes the counterimage of the Machine as an active force in Wright's work—evidenced from early days in Wright's famous talk on that theme. Well and good, we can accept an interpretation of Fallingwater as part Nature and part Machine, but here, it seems to me, is where Thomas H. Beeby's paper is so moving.

All of a sudden we are drowned in Nature, swept into the Driftless Area of southern Wisconsin. The prairie floods in from Illinois; the rivers scour their beds, hollowing out the valleys, throwing up long shining bars of sand. Culture is not excluded. Myth peoples the landscape with divinity. We are with Wright as he grows up in that landscape. We run with him through heavy meadows and pause to look at our image in the stream. Shadowy, the prairie houses take shape around us, their spaces flowing through them and out in a heavy current, their masonry water-scoured in long horizontal striations, the heavy roofs of summer pressing down. We are convinced. It is a magnificent tour de force on Beeby's part. Is it true? The question need hardly arise, since in art so many incompatible things are usually all true together. It is a great myth, one of the greatest yet woven about

Wright, worthy of him and of the young generation of architects in Chicago, of whom Beeby is one, who have opened as warmly to him as to Mies van der Rohe.

Into this dichotomy between Nature and abstraction steps Neil Levine's paper, which brilliantly reconciles the two conceptions, or states of being. Levine shows how the abstraction of Sullivan and Wright was itself involved with natural associations—necessarily so, insofar as it had jettisoned the associational imagery of existent architectural styles. He outlines Wright's dilemma around 1909, when, in Levine's view, he had carried abstraction as far as it could go *toward Nature*, and so had to break away from it to find a way, through "representation," to come back at Nature once again. This is an astute perception, and Levine develops it in a highly convincing way throughout his analysis of Wright's later work. Indeed, Levine defines the character of the decisive joint in Wright's design around 1910 more perceptively than anyone else has yet done, and from that perception the power of the rest of his argument derives. The first Taliesin emerges as the first of the new, more wholly representational order. The tragedy which took place there is embodied by Levine in appropriately architectural terms, as Wright moves "The Flower in the Crannied Wall" from its triumphant position on the hilltop to its last resting place below ground. A pity Wright's body could not have been left in peace there too, as he wanted it to be.

Levine then examines the desert dwellings and develops the concept of the container, which was in fact to dominate the later decades of Wright's life. The pot, the cistern, the Amerindian basket, and, though Levine does not pursue them, the goddess temples of Malta built into the earth—the enclosed circles and the labyrinth—all play their part in that search for "great peace" which formed Wright's last years. Finally, of course, Levine deals with Taliesin West, with its echo of the landscape and its evocations of human history in the desert, and, at last, with Marin County, where the forms of Rome which Wright had, perhaps perforce, rejected in his youth were subverted by him—or perhaps returned to their ultimate origins—in the stretched aqueducts of the County Center and the low, landscape-evoking profile of its dome.

So Levine in his own way shows us two Wrights, or two different epochs of Wright, the second growing naturally enough out of the structure of the first. Donald Hoffman's paper, *Meeting Nature Face to Face,* is less specific. It is perhaps more an expression of pious hope than an analysis of the way Nature is concretely embodied in Wright's architectural forms. Still, it opens with an impassioned statement worth quoting in part: "Academic art history," Hoffman writes, "almost never bothers with nature. . . . Art is presumed to nourish itself on previous art, which the historian thus researches, routinely and obsessively, for the presumed 'sources.' These habits of academic scholarship reduce the creative act to something hardly worth studying. A source as manifold and marvelous as nature finds almost no currency in the intellectual world." Alas, art does in fact come out of art to a perhaps surprising degree in human history. At the same time, we have seen that natural analogies are essential to Wright's work. It would be absurd to overlook them. But it is equally ridiculous to ignore the other side of Wright, the one that got him started time after time: his ability to learn from architectural culture.

Of all modern architects Wright was the richest in the breadth of his borrowings across time and among the most determined to conceal them. I began this introduction by suggesting that Wright had indeed concealed a major source of his strength from his apprentices: his capacity to "condense" the work of others into a "new unity." On this issue all the other papers in this group have been silent, while Hoffman rushes loyally out to do battle with the ogre. So it is precisely this aspect of Wright, a central one, that is absent in this series, and perhaps from most of the scholarship on Wright being done at the present time. For that reason, if for no other, a stenographic outline of Wright's marvelous condensations may not be out of order as a conclusion to this introduction and as a complement to the other essays.* A course can be set from one representative monument to the next, though many others might be singled out as well.

*Developed in detail in my *Frank Lloyd Wright,* New York, 1960, and in my keynote address at the symposium on Fallingwater held at the Buell Center, Columbia University, November 1986, now in process of publication.

INTRODUCTION

1. Wright's own house of 1889 condenses three houses by Bruce Price at Tuxedo Park, of 1885–86, which themselves show decisive influences from Mayan architecture as published by Charnay in 1885, leading to:

2. The Charnley house, of 1891, which grafts the mask of the Mayan rain god, Tlaloc, onto a Froebel block as an entrance, leading to:

3. The Winslow house, of 1893, which combines its mask-of-Tlaloc entrance door and windows with a serpent doorway out of Catherwood and the general massing of the Turkish pavilion at the Columbian Exposition of 1893.

4. The project for the Milwaukee Museum, of 1893, adapts Perrault's east front of the Louvre along lines suggested by Charles Atwood's Fine Arts Building at the Exposition.

5. The Ward Willitts house, of 1902, follows the River Forest Golf Club of 1898 in adapting the hipped roof over continuous windows of Voysey's Broadleys on Lake Windermere of 1898, but develops a new space like that suggested in Beeby's landscape analogy, though deriving in large part from the Shingle Style and its Colonial Revival and Japanese components. Most of the Prairie School houses derive from these condensations.

6. The Heurtley house, of 1902, adapts Lutyens's Deanery Gardens at Sonning, of 1900–1901, and recasts it into a form evoking natural shapes, especially those of mountain and cavern; all this culminating in the Robie house's condensation in 1909 of sacred mountain and airplane.

7. In more cubical buildings a line can be traced from Voysey's Grey house in Bedford Park, of 1888–91, through Olbrich's Habisch house at Darmstadt, of 1901, to Wright's Fricke house, of 1902. This line culminates in:

8. The Larkin Building, of 1904, whose major model is the Secession Building in Vienna, of 1896–99, by Olbrich. The ball-in-the-box of the first Froebel "gift" appears in the Secession Building and crowns the piers of the Larkin Building, which also suggests the prints of Gothic cathedrals Wright's mother placed in his room. The space suggests the Jungian "Death-and-Resurrection" archetype and is again all Wright's own, the greatest architectural embodiment of the Romantic "quest."

9. In Unity Temple, of 1906, the Secession Building and the Froebel cube are again the models, but the same Death-and-Resurrection progression leads to the meeting room, which suggests the Neoplatonic man-centered structure of the universe, to which the little building seems to release its occupants.

10. Midway Gardens, of 1914, adapts Olbrich's Studios at Darmstadt of c. 1900 with their sculpture. Olbrich's arch appears inside. Wright was called "the American Olbrich" when he visited Germany in 1909.

11. Taliesin at Spring Green, of 1911–14, puts everything together in a newly natural way, embracing the hilltop.

12. The Richland Center Warehouse, of 1915, is closely based on the Temple of the Three Lintels at Chichén Itzá.

13. The Barnsdall house, of 1920, suggests Structure 33 at Yaxchilan, especially in Beaux-Arts reconstruction.

14. The Millard house, of 1923, abstracts the masks of Tlaloc into structural blocks; its massing closely follows that of Le Corbusier's project for his Maison Citrohan with pilotis, published in 1922.

15. The Richard Lloyd Jones house at Tulsa, of 1929, condenses the project for a brick country house by Mies van der Rohe, of 1922, and his Wolf house at Guben, of 1927.

16. The Goetsch-Winkler house, of 1939, and, indeed, most of the Usonians, beginning with the Jacobs house of 1937, combine the Barcelona Pavilion by Mies with numerous Amerindian details and Wright's "natural" imagery.

17. Fallingwater, of 1936–37, derives indirectly from the Villa Savoie and Dutch Neoplasticism and directly from Schindler's Lovell house of 1927 and Neutra's Lovell house of 1929–30. Amerindian pyramidal massing is essential to it and, as always, the concordance between sacred mountain and airplane. Despite its small size, it is—like the Parthenon, Hagia Sophia, and Chartres—one of the mightiest condensations of opposites in all architecture.

18. The Johnson Wax Building, of 1936–39, combines the "waterglass" exterior Wright spoke of so often in later life with the interior column, as do the neolithic goddess temples on Malta, creating the Death-and-Resurrection archetype in female form. Wright called it the

feminine counterpart of the masculine Larkin Building. The Jester project, of 1938–40, continues the type, which culminates in, among other buildings:

19. The Guggenheim Museum, of 1946–59, which employs the labyrinth as well, and also recalls Mono's stairway in the Vatican of 1932.

20. The Church of the Annunciation at Wauwatosa, designed at the end of Wright's life, employs the peristyle in the Flavian palace on the Palatine and in the "Maritime Theater" in Hadrian's Villa to support a dome.

21. The Administration Building for Marin County, of 1959, combines aqueduct and dome.

22. Florida Southern College, of 1938–59, closely adapts the plan of Hadrian's Villa at Tivoli.

23. Taliesin West, of 1936ff., combines pre-Columbian imitation of mountain profile and horizontal compressive lines, as at Teotihuacán, with a simplification of Hadrian's Villa in plan. The monument to Wright's stepdaughter in the loggia derives from Lutyens's fountains at New Delhi, as does the Huntington Hartford project of 1948—all of these deriving in the end from Indian lily-pad garden motifs, to which the columns of the Johnson Wax Building are also connected.

It is no wonder that Wright has as yet no progeny. The enormous cultural condensation, the new unity, he represented is not at all imitable and will probably not soon come again. So the best of the younger architects, such as Robert Venturi, have tried to start back where Wright began and to move from there to the Shingle Style vernacular from which he sprang. And Beeby, building a house on the prairie in Wisconsin, reflects in it not Wright's second Herbert Jacobs house, which is dug into the earth in a perfect enactment of Beeby's prose, but the tall, thin wooden vernacular of the region. Beeby's culture is different. The Swedish sod houses on the prairie can have been known to him only through literary references. Wright must have seen them. But the reasons lie deeper. The younger architects seek contextuality, not originality; their instinct is to enshrine historical culture rather than to plunder it. For all of their love of the landscape, they are men of the modern city; they cannot, like Wright, cast it aside. So Wright is still far from us, born of an older world. Perhaps these essays will help bring him closer, charged with some ancient secrets of creation and of our land.

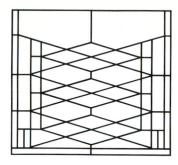

WRIGHT ON NATURE AND THE MACHINE

JOSEPH CONNORS

In nineteenth-century American art and literature the machine and the natural environment made uneasy bedfellows. Machines like locomotives, steamboats, reapers, and spinning mills invaded the primeval American garden and shattered the pastoral ideal. The train that ran along the edge of Walden Pond interrupted Thoreau's silent communion with nature: "The whistle of the locomotive penetrates my woods summer and winter, sounding like the scream of a hawk sailing over some farmer's yard. . . . [The clouds of smoke] rising higher and higher, going to heaven while the cars are going to Boston, conceals the sun for a minute and casts my distant fields into shade."[1] Leo Marx has called the tension between the technological and the natural "the root conflict of our culture." Barbara Novak has shown how the Claudian pastoral conventions of mid-nineteenth-century American landscape painting were adapted either to mute the presence of locomotives in landscapes or to heighten the sense of their alien presence and looming threat.[2]

Other currents of American thought celebrated the machine and developed an aesthetic theory around it. The sculptor Horatio Greenough (1805–52) used the examples of the American trotting wagon and the warship to explore the impact of function on machine design. His famous motto Greek Principles Not Greek Things carried the functional aesthetic into the realm of architecture. The static perfection of Greek or Greek Revival architecture was contrasted with the dynamic evolution of a machine grappling with its task. The perceptive architect would henceforth master principles rather than imitate dead forms. Greenough defined "Beauty as the promise of Function; Action as the presence of Function; Character as the record of Function." Machines, tested in do-or-die situations and worn by continual use, had a cold, hard beauty all their own:

> If we compare the form of a newly invented machine with the perfected type of the same instrument, we observe, as we trace it through the phases of improvement, how weight is shaken off where strength is less needed, how functions are made to approach without impeding each other, how straight becomes curved, and the curve is straightened, till the straggling and cumbersome machine becomes the compact, effective, and beautiful engine.[3]

Wright was heir to this native functionalist tradition, and an echo of Greenough can be heard in the verses which he chose to inscribe on the balcony of the Oak Park drafting room:

> An' by that light now mark my word
> We'll build the perfect ship.[4]

It is as though Wright's assistants and apprentices were being trained as shipwrights of the new architecture, of the sloops and schooners that the Prairie school was launching to replace the galleons and men-of-war of the Richardsonian era. But simultaneously Wright was heir to a tradition of American naturalism that he himself traced back to Emerson as well as to his boyhood experiences in Spring Green. Tensions there might well be between these two legacies, but Wright's thinking was resilient enough to hold both in balance and to explore links between them. His vision of nature emphasizes its abstract and even mathematical qualities, while his vision of the machine is highly organic and biomorphic. His houses are machines that have taken root in nature or that are metamorphosing into gardens. Fashions of interpretation that sever these two realms are likely to be misleading, whether they exalt Wright as the high priest of a mystic return to nature, or see him as the isolated American prophet of the European Machine Age.

WRIGHT ON NATURE AND THE MACHINE

In this essay I would like to examine the classic moment of 1900–1901 when images of nature and of the machine were given their most powerful expressions in Wright's writings. I would also like to assert that this marriage of symbolic worlds was to remain fundamental in Wright's later thought and design. In particular, it conditioned his response in the 1930s to the International style, which he felt to be, simultaneously, attractive because of its machine imagery and repulsive because of its neglect of nature. The equilibrium Wright felt he had achieved in the Prairie House was disturbed by European modernism, but he managed to retrieve it in his design for the Kaufmann house at Bear Run in 1935. Fallingwater, Wright's polemic response to modernism, arises from the ideas and imagery that flowed in such profusion from his pen and pencil in the years around 1900.

NATURE

The most eloquent expression of Wright's early ideas on nature is found in an article written in 1900 by Robert C. Spencer.[5] Spencer was a young architect who came under Wright's spell, absorbed his ideas, and even imitated his style of dress. The photographs and drawings in Spencer's article come directly from Wright, and we can assume that the ideas do as well, and probably much of the actual language. Spencer's main theme is that in Wright's work there is no firm line between nature and art:

> [Wright had a] sympathy with nature, a natural sympathy developed by early training, the wise accentuation of early tastes and tendencies by his mother, and seasons of young manhood spent at Hillside farm among the woods and fields of Wisconsin; a sympathy which subsequent technical training failed to impair. You do not feel that these buildings have been dropped accidentally upon the ground or into holes in the earth dug carelessly. The artificial structure reaches out and fraternizes with the natural environment, inviting flower and vine in turn to clamber over walls and flourish within curb of brick and stone, each mingling with each. There is a formality in these arrangements, but it is a simple broad formality which avoids the hard and labored artificiality which has done so much to discredit the formal garden among

lovers of nature. There is no painfully hard and fast line between nature and art, there is no mutilation of the one to bring it into a forced correspondence with the other. (p. 66).

Creative contact with nature takes a very special kind of education. Spencer is the first to mention Wright's exposure as a child in the Boston area to Froebel's system of kindergarten education but he goes on to add that it was the apprenticeship with Sullivan, whom he calls "an independent and close student of nature" (p. 69), that showed Wright the true possibilities of a natural architecture.

At this point in the development of Wright's thought, nature wears two very different faces. The first is that of an abundant, prolific, tangled nature; the second, conventionalized, geometric, and abstract. As Robert Spencer put it, "Nature, who knows the most rigid and subtle geometry, as well as the most voluptuous freedom of, and apparent confusion of form, is the source to which he has always gone for inspiration" (p. 69). Confused and voluptuous nature recalls the famous image of the tangled bank with which Darwin ends the *Origin of Species:*

> It is interesting to contemplate an entangled bank, clothed with many plants of many kinds, with birds singing on the bushes, with various insects flitting about, and with worms crawling through the damp earth, and to reflect that these elaborately constructed forms, so different from each other, and dependent on each other in so complex a manner, have all been produced by laws acting around us . . . from so simple a beginning endless forms most beautiful and most wonderful have been, and are being evolved.[6]

More Darwinian still is the image of the plumed bird that Robert Spencer employs:

> A face to be beautiful need not be muscular, hard and bony, it need not merely be anatomical in its outward aspect. While it is true that in a building form should follow function, the proposition is true only in its larger sense, in the sense in which it is exemplified in nature, who always seeks to clothe the working

mechanism of her organisms beneath a protective covering none the less fair or beautiful because fitted to its purpose. The sticklers for naked cast-iron in facades of modern construction would do well to contrast the plumaged bird with the plucked and naked specimen, and that in turn with the bony skeleton. (p. 68).

Out of Darwin, filtered through Sullivan, comes the idea of a voluptuously creative, plumed, entangled nature. But rising to discipline, it is a more geometrical and abstract nature, "a Nature who knows the most rigid and subtle geometry." The young Wright clutched at geometry precisely because he could not draw, at least not up to Sullivan's standard. He said of his apprenticeship:

> Beginning at the drawing board it was my natural tendency to draw away from the mastery of his effloresence toward the straight line and rectangular pattern, working my own rectilinear way with T-square and triangle toward the more severe rhythms of point, line and plane. Never having been a painter I had never drawn more than a little 'freehand.' . . . my technique condemned me to T-square and triangle, which I came to love and prefer, but they compelled me to stay behind the sensuous expressions the master so much loved.[7]

Wright was also, consciously or unconsciously, declaring allegiance to an age-old Platonic tradition of Nature the mathematician, a tradition that was explored by the seventeenth-century botanist Nehemiah Grew ("from the contemplation of Plants, men might first be invited to Mathematical Enquirys"),[8] advanced by nineteenth-century ornamentalists like Owen Jones[9] and Ruprich Robert,[10] and given its definitive formulation in the great 1917 book by English botanist D'Arcy Wentworth Thompson, *On Growth and Form*.[11] Nature the voluptuous and nature the severely mathematical: there is a creative tension set up between these two poles in Spencer's article, and also, when one looks for it, in Wright's early houses.

The Winslow house in River Forest was Wright's first commission after his break with Sullivan and in many ways his first Natural House. It is famous for doing homage to the tall elm that stood on the lot before

Winslow acquired it. In Spencer's words: "Upon the chosen site Nature has been at work for years building the wonderful elm, which, with its spreading arms and feathery sprays, was destined to shade this house, and the character of the house was somewhat determined by the circumstance of this tree" (p. 66). The idea may have been sparked by a McKim, Mead, and White house of a decade earlier, the Misses Appleton house of 1883, which was built in a horseshoe shape to spare the magnificent elm seen in Sheldon's early photograph.[12] But Wright took the tree image much more seriously and let it permeate to the inner core of his design. The house became a conventionalized metaphor for natural growth, though not a literal imitation of a tree. The rise of the walls from the stylobate up to the foliate frieze under the overhanging eaves is described as a "beginning, an upward growth, and an ending."[13] The color scheme as described by Spencer was less somber than it is now:

> The softly mottled bricks range from a golden tan to a deep, ruddy orange, while the roof tiles were a special burning which produced an indescribable surface-tone approaching a soft salmon color. Frieze of dull tan, wood mouldings of brown, and eaves of golden yellow, throwing their reflected light into the upper casements, are the elements of the color scheme. (p. 71).

We are reminded of the Monadnock Building, which, as Donald Hoffmann discovered, was originally designed with bricks that would lighten as the building rose from brown at the bottom to yellow at the top, reinforcing the impression that the structure was an organic growth out of the swampy subsoil of the Chicago plain.[14] And the image of growth is beautifully expressed in the conventionalized tree of the Winslow front door, with its long mathematical trunk and burst of Sullivanesque foliage at the top. At the rear of the house the T-shaped plan allows the rooms to mingle more freely with the out-of-doors: a large tree trunk was left standing on one side of the dining room, and on the other side an octagonal staircase, with Gothic tracery, acts as pendant, a metaphor for a natural trunk. It is as though the courtyard side of Glessner house had been depotted from its cramped urban

WRIGHT ON NATURE AND THE MACHINE

environment and rerooted in the suburbs, where it had room to grow and breathe.

The natural metaphors in the Winslow house should not let us forget that Wright was also grappling with architectural precedents, both distant, like the classic temples to which Spencer compares the profiles and mouldings of the house (p. 64), and immediate, like the work that was coming out of Sullivan's office when Wright left it. Sullivan's Victoria Hotel of 1892 would have suggested the idea of a dematerialized frieze zone separating the mass of the building from the hovering roof.[15] And of course Sullivan's Wainwright tomb of 1892 suggested the band of ornament that locks door and windows into a central unit, and the urns, blocks, and other outworks that bind the Winslow house to its sidewalk.[16] We should also not forget that Wright let similar ideas mature simultaneously in several different designs. For example, an unexecuted project for the Peter Goan house of 1893–94 closely resembles the Winslow house,[17] though it is fussier than its twin in its treatment of the corners, and it has not quite yet fused into the cohesive Winslow block.

The Chauncey Williams house of 1894 was built a few lots away from the Winslow house by clients in the same social circle.[18] Its steep-pitched roof, like a Euclidean abstraction of a Loire château roof, was not much repeated and has made the house appear eccentric within Wright's oeuvre. Indeed, it makes one think of the passage in the *Autobiography* that describes Wright's Welsh ancestor who sold felt hats at country fairs, hats steeply pointed like witches' bonnets, tough enough to walk on (p. 25). But the podium of the Williams house, built of Roman brick over boulders dredged out of the bed of the Des Plaines River by the Winslows, Williamses, and Wrights, shows that the guiding idea of the design is "the House not built with human hands" described in *The House Beautiful* of 1896–97:

A bit of pavement from Pompei, a fragment from the pyramids, is prized because man's touch was on it 2000 or thrice 2000 years ago; but each pebble in the chinks of the cellar-wall beneath us holds thousands of thousands of years locked up in it, since first the ancient oceans sifted it and inner earth baked it and thickening continents began to squeeze it into rock.[19]

But the Williams house is also a symbolic response to a famous late design by Richardson, the Ames Gate Lodge of 1880.[20] Richardson used massive boulders to suggest a building that was more a glacial deposit than a structure made by human hands, but the upper stories of the bedroom and well-tower are given French Renaissance detailing, as though to suggest a metaphor of civilization resting on its sub-civilized or primeval base. Richardson underlines the fragility of the superstructure; Wright celebrates it. The Williams house becomes the Natural House par excellence, "not built by human hands," but "thought-built" and capped by a statement of the abstracting powers of the human mind.

The key link between these early Natural Houses and the mature Prairie House is the Heller house of 1898.[21] Thanks to a drawing originally published by Spencer and recently sold in New York, we can see the design in evolution.[22] The drawing is as colorful as a bright Monet watercolor, with green and red flowers and a bright orange tile roof like the one the Winslow house originally had. The original scheme called for a central pavilion three stories high, flanked by lower wings, bounded by attached octagonal columns, and full of Gothic ornament. In overall plan it looks like two Winslow barns set at right angles to form an L. The final house follows the original plan and is still three stories high, but a few subtle changes have been introduced that make the house seem more horizontal and prairie-hugging. The octagonal piers are gone; the roof of the side wings cuts across the central block; there are two dematerialized zones that make the roofs appear to hover as though over a void. The floral ornament around the door and the frieze of dancing youths by Richard Bock are still a tribute to Sullivan (and perhaps beyond him to Donatello), but otherwise we seem to have crossed some invisible threshold, from the Wright of the nineteenth to the Wright of the twentieth century. The Gothic house of the drawing has metamorphosed into a fine-tooled machine.

WRIGHT ON NATURE AND THE MACHINE

The ideals informing Wright's machine aesthetic would be spelled out a few years after the Heller house and just a year after Spencer's article in Wright's famous speech of 1901, "The Art and Craft of the Machine."[23] When it was first delivered to the Arts and Crafts Society of Chicago, it had a defiant ring. Disciples of Ruskin and Morris were told that "in the machine lies the only future of art and craft," and that "the Machine is the metamorphosis of ancient art and craft" (p. 65). But what did Wright mean by the machine? When one analyzes the imagery of the speech, most of the examples of machines and machine processes are familiar from Wright's own experience. He was not just preaching but speaking from his own attempts as an artist to confront the machine.

Wright mentioned woodcutting machines and mechanized furniture production. When one looks at his own furniture, one sees the symbiosis of machine tools and meticulous craftsmanship.[24] Another mechanical process he mentioned is electrogalvanizing. Here he could draw on the experience of his friend and patron William Winslow, who made his fortune in the production of ornamental iron treated with a variety of newly invented electroplating processes.[25] The Winslow Brothers trade catalog of 1893 shows some of the firm's prestigious productions: the iron stairways of the Rookery, of the Armour Institute, and of the Mills Building in San Francisco; and an array of street lamps, safes, drinking fountains, door knockers, and andirons in a broad spectrum of styles. More than any other firm, it was the Winslow Brothers who turned the commercial elevator into an aerial cage and raised it to the level of a work of art. Winslow was the man who did the ironwork for the Auditorium Building, and it was at that site that he met Sullivan's young draftsman, Wright, ten years his junior, and the author of many of the drawings that he would turn into ornamental iron. Their friendship led of course to the Winslow house, and inevitably Wright included ornamental iron as part of the design.

Another machine image mentioned by Wright's speech is the skyscraper: "The tall modern office building is the machine pure and simple." Here Wright shows himself a true disciple of Sullivan and a close reader of Sullivan's essay "The Tall Office Building Artistically

Considered,"[26] where the mechanical systems of the skyscraper are elevated to symbolic, almost mystic importance.

But the machine that dominates the imagery of the speech is the printing press. In 1901 Wright was under the influence of Whistler's lithographs, which had been exhibited the year before by the Caxton Club, of which Wright was a member, at the Art Institute of Chicago: "That delicate thing, the lithograph—the prince of a whole reproductive province of processes—see what this process becomes in the hands of a master like Whistler. He has sounded but one note in the gamut of its possibilities, but that product is intrinsically true to the process, and as delicate as the butterfly's wing."[27] There must have been other things that attracted Wright to Whistler, who was an early collector of Japanese prints and oriental porcelain, who dressed exotically, who built a home and studio based on principles of simplicity and lightness with decoration in an oriental vein. Wright would not have been in much sympathy with Whistler's creed of Art for Art's Sake, but he would have appreciated the lyric transformation of an industrial landscape that one finds in Whistler's *Nocturne* lithographs of the Thames at Battersea, at a time "when the evening mist clothes the riverside with poetry, as with a veil, and the poor buildings lose themselves in the dim sky, and the tall chimneys become campanili, and the warehouses are palaces in the night."[28]

Whistler was an interesting contemporary, but for Wright the great mythographer of the printing press was Victor Hugo. Hugo's *Notre Dame de Paris* had stirred Wright's imagination since boyhood and is quoted at length in "The Art and Craft of the Machine."[29] Why was Wright so impressed with Victor Hugo? First, because Hugo was a towering figure in French architectural thought, a founder of Gothic archeology and grandfather to a generation of Gothic revivalists. But more specifically, because Hugo served as a vital link between Wright's two passions, printing and architecture. In chapters added to the eighth edition (1832) of *Notre Dame,* probably with the advice of the archeologist Charles Robelin and possibly after criticism by the young Henri Labrouste, Hugo outlined a theory which is a direct ancestor of the kind of thinking elaborated in Elizabeth Eisenstein's recent work on the printing revolution.[30] The monk Claude Frollo is having a talk with

WRIGHT ON NATURE AND THE MACHINE

the king of France in his cell overlooking the gigantic cathedral. Frollo wistfully points to the one printed book among the many manuscripts in his cell (an innocuous commentary on St. Paul's epistles), and then leans to look out on Notre Dame and says mysteriously, "This will kill that. . . . Small things overcome great ones. . . . The Nile rat kills the crocodile, the swordfish kills the whale, the book will kill the building."

Hugo's theory is that architecture, from the birth of civilization to the eve of the Gutenberg era, was the great book of mankind, the one outlet of true genius. Anyone who was born a poet became an architect. The *Iliads* of the culture took the form of cathedrals. Ideas in manuscripts perished, but great buildings survived. After the invention of the printing press, genius turned to the printed book, and the life-blood ebbed out of architecture. From the Renaissance onward, architecture was sick and dying: "It dragged on, like a pitiable mendicant of the studios from imitation to imitation" while "the press waxed and grew fat."

It was Hugo who taught Wright to despise architecture based on revival styles, to scorn the Renaissance as "the setting sun which we take to be a dawn." He also taught him to see the architect as the poet in stone, the leader who orchestrates all of the other arts under his direction. And of course he taught him the importance of the printing press, even for an architect whose sad fate was to live four hundred years after Gutenberg.

The "Art and Craft of the Machine" closes with a powerful extended metaphor, the great industrial city (Chicago, one supposes) as a monstrous organic machine:

> Be gently lifted up at nightfall to the top of a great down-town office building, and you may see how in the image of material man, at once his glory and menace, is this thing we call a city.
>
> There beneath, grown up in a night, is the monster leviathan, stretching acre upon acre into the far distance. High overhead hangs the stagnant pall of its fetid breath, reddened with the light from its myriad eyes endlessly everywhere blinking. Ten thousand acres of cellular tissue, layer upon layer, the city's flesh, outspreads enmeshed by intricate network of veins and arteries,

radiating into the gloom, and there with muffled, persistent roar, pulses and circulates as the blood in your veins, the ceaseless beat of the activity to whose necessities it all conforms.

. . . Its nerve ganglia!—The peerless Corliss tandems[31] whirling their hundred ton fly-wheels, fed by gigantic rows of water tube boilers burning oil, a solitary man slowly pacing backward and forward, regulating here and there the little feed valves controlling the deafening roar of the flaming gas, while beyond, the incessant clicking, dropping, waiting-lifting, waiting, shifting of the governor gear controlling these modern Goliaths seems a visible brain in intelligent action, registered infallibly in the enormous magnets, purring in the giant embrace of great induction coils, generating the vital current meeting with instant response in the rolling cars on elevated tracks ten miles away, where the glare of the Bessemer steel converter makes a conflagration of the clouds. (Pp. 72–73)

Possibly inspired by the chapter in *Notre Dame* titled "A Bird's-Eye View of Paris," Wright's "Chicago à vol d'oiseau" is almost closer to Fritz Lang's *Metropolis*. The industrial city is the ultimate machine, but at the same time it is the ultimate organism, a leviathan with circulatory system, nerve ganglia, and brain. Wright's critics of the 1930s would accuse him of abandoning the city for a pastoral utopia, but they forgot this powerful, bizarre image of 1901, in which the two worlds of machine and natural organism merge.

EPILOGUE

The ideas of nature and the machine that Wright so vigorously studied around 1900 returned later in different contexts to cross-fertilize each other and to provide fresh sources for his thinking. New machines like the automobile came to enrich his repertoire of images and experience. His projects of 1924 for an "automobile objective" at Sugarloaf Mountain near Washington, D.C., rely on the assumption that future experience of nature will be primarily automotive. He felt that the automobile had fundamentally changed our perception of space, and when his client, Gordon Strong, rejected his projects, Wright complained that any other design would leave the car "betrayed and aban-

WRIGHT ON NATURE AND THE MACHINE

doned as usual." The same project shows his fascination with other new machines, such as dirigibles, which were to anchor at a mooring mast atop Wright's spiral, and the new Zeiss projection apparatus, the world's first planetarium, that had just been unveiled in Munich.

Alongside his fascination with new machines lay a growing unease about the new machine architecture. This was the period when Wright was grappling with the challenge of International modernism. He was annoyed that a historiography of modern architecture had grown up that relegated him to the position of a grandfather of the modern movement, a prophet who had charted the course in the early days but who like Moses would never himself enter the Promised Land. History had made of him a great romantic: "Romantic too are the reminiscences of older forms, from exotic cultures of the East, which still survive in his imagination and in his buildings."[33] But the watchword of the new style was discipline, and the architectural movements of the day, like the political movements sweeping Europe, had no room for the maverick. From his own point of view, Wright saw the Europeans as former allies who had gone to extremes, leaving out what was human, romantic, and dramatic from their buildings, but also making off with forms and ideas Wright considered his own.

The polemic between Wright and the International movement was worked out in the periodical *T-Square* (soon renamed *Shelter*) in the early months of 1932.[34] *T-Square* was a new and progressive magazine from Philadelphia that generally favored European modernism and featured it in articles by or about Richard Neutra, Mies van der Rohe, Philip Johnson, George Howe, and Henry-Russell Hitchcock. In an article of that year by Norman Rice, photographs that show the main currents within the movement are juxtaposed. Corbusier's Villa Stein is the crown prince, a transition toward the architecture of tomorrow. But competing with Corbusier on the left, so to speak, is Buckminster Fuller, whose extensive and inimitable writings are printed in every issue and whose famous Dymaxion house of 1929 is shown frequently in photographs.[35] Fuller attacked what he called the "quasi functional style" and predicted that "the International Mode must perish, being eclectic rather than scientific, science being the Life Blood of Function" (p. 35). The true machine dwelling, the Ford of housing, was his prototype house, anchored to the ground "with the sturdiness of a giant redwood," suspended from a mooring mast, providing total mechanical services and a completely controlled environment, to the point that "No bed clothes or other clothes are necessary for comfort." But if mainstream modernism was challenged from the left by Fuller, it was also challenged from the other direction by Wright, whose Taliesin is displayed in Rice's article with the caption: "Protest—And the first theses of a new architecture." Wright too criticized the Europeans for a new breed of eclecticism. The machine was important but not everything, and if America was not careful it might "by way of machine worship, go machine mad"[36] (here he probably means Fuller). As for Le Corbusier, whose recent work had been lavishly illustrated in *T-Square* as well as in the International Style exhibition at the Museum of Modern Art in New York, Wright had already expressed his opinion in his review of *Towards a New Architecture* in 1928. Le Corbusier was all right as far as he went, but the trouble was that he left out the third dimension, depth, the essential complement of surface and mass, depth "that alone can give life or purpose to the other two dimensions and result in that integrity in Architecture that makes the building no less organic than the tree itself."[37]

It takes an effort of the imagination to see how Wright felt about European modernism, but the effort can be aided by looking at the photographs available to him in journals like *T-Square*. The new buildings seemed to him to lack depth, to lack heart, to lack romance. They were supposed to resemble machines, which to Wright was like saying that the heart was just a suction pump. He argued that "our architecture itself would become a poor, flat-faced thing of steel-bones, box-outlines, gas-pipe and hand-rail fittings . . . without this essential *heart* beating in it."[38] If he had been able to see Le Corbusier's drawings for the Villa Stein, or if he had looked carefully at the model in the Museum of Modern Art, he would have seen the immense effort Le Corbusier had made to pack a set of rambling terraces (as shown in the early drawings) into a dense and thoughtful cube, one that had depth and adventure built deep inside it. But to Wright the Villa Stein was just another cardboard house.[39] It was the basic idea of his "Art and Craft" lecture of 1901 taken to an absurd extreme at the expense of nature and other fundamental values. As Wright looked over the pages of *T-Square* he began to dream of a house that could incorporate concrete cantilevered terraces with all the depth and romance that Le Corbusier's architecture lacked, a house that would combine machine forms with Taliesin's rustic stonework, with the imagery of the "House not built by human hands" but rather assembled out of rocks deposited at the beginning of geological time. Nature and the machine had fused in Wright's early writings, and he was groping for the formula that would allow them to fuse again in a house. At this point the Kaufmanns came on the scene.

It is now a well-known anecdote that Wright designed Fallingwater in 1935 in the few hours that elapsed between a phone call from Edgar Kaufmann, Sr., saying that he was about to leave Milwaukee by car, and his arrival later that day at Taliesin.[40] The story may well be true, but Wright could put the preliminary plan of Fallingwater on paper that fast because he had been designing this house in his mind ever since he had looked over the spread of photographs in *T-Square* in 1932.

Wright had long known what he wanted: a house made up of concrete terraces exploding from a central core. (The idea of "explosion" was important; after all, Hitchcock and Johnson had said that Wright had dynamited the box of the traditional house.[41]) But he also wanted rustic stonework that reached back, metaphorically, to Taliesin and past it to the boulders of the Chauncey Williams house, the Ames Gate Lodge, and the nature of Emerson and Olmsted. These elements, however, had to have the third dimension that European modernism lacked, so Wright continued to refine the design of Fallingwater. He elongated the terraces and added various "aerofoil" planes to the chimney to accentuate the feeling of motion, and he opened up the chimney core until it became a three-story tower anchoring the terraces and catching the perspective view from downstream. In fact, the early design was tested and refined by the device of "perspective proof" that had been used years before to breathe more depth and drama into the Robie house.[42] All these changes brought a depth and a three-dimensionality to the house that no International style building seemed to have, and with these qualities came a deep symbolism of romance in a supremely natural setting. The Prairie House up to 1910 was "married to the ground,"[43] but the Kaufmann house had eloped with a waterfall. Wright's polemic against his former allies of modernism remained shrill and sterile so long as it was confined to the pages of the architectural journals, but it made him think once again about the old antithesis between nature and machine that he had overcome around 1900, and it eventually led him to Fallingwater, the Natural House for the Machine Age.

NOTES

1. Quoted in Leo Marx, *The Machine in the Garden: Technology and the Pastoral Ideal in America.* (London: Oxford University Press, 1964), 250–51.

2. Barbara Novak, *Nature and Culture: American Landscapes and Painting, 1825–1875* (New York: Oxford University Press, 1980), 166–84.

3. Horatio Greenough, *Form and Function: Remarks on Art, Design, and Architecture,* ed. Harold Small (Berkeley: University of California Press, 1947), 59, 71.

4. *Frank Lloyd Wright: Ausgeführte Bauten* (Berlin; Ernst Wasmuth, 1911); reprinted as *Frank Lloyd Wright: The Early Work* (New York: Horizon Press, 1968), fig. 108.

5. Robert C. Spencer, Jr., "The Work of Frank Lloyd Wright," *Architectural Review* (Boston) 7 (June 1900): 61–72; facsimile ed. (Park Forest, Ill.: Prairie School Press, 1964).

6. Charles Darwin, *The Origin of Species,* quoted in Howard E. Gruber, *Darwin on Man: A Psychological Study of Scientific Creativity,* 2nd ed. (Chicago: University of Chicago Press, 1981), 106–7.

7. Frank Lloyd Wright, *Genius and the Mobocracy* (1949; New York: Horizon Press, 1971), 71.

8. Nehemiah Grew, *The Anatomy of Plants* (London, 1682); reprint with an Introduction by Conway Zirkle (New York, 1965), 152.

9. Owen Jones, *The Grammar of Ornament* (London, 1856). Wright cites this as one of the books he borrowed from the library of the All Souls Unitarian Church, along with Viollet-le-Duc's *Habitations of Man in All Ages;* see Frank Lloyd Wright, *An Autobiography* (1932; New York: Horizon Press, 1977), 97, 113.

10. Victor Marie Charles Ruprich Robert, *Flore ornementale* (Paris, 1876). For Ruprich Robert's debt to Viollet-le-Duc, see Barry Bergdoll, "'The Synthesis of All I Have Seen': The Architecture of Edmont Duthoit, 1837–89," in

WRIGHT ON NATURE AND THE MACHINE

Robin Middleton, ed., *The Beaux-Arts and Nineteenth-Century French Architecture* (London: Thames and Hudson, 1982), 221.

Suggestive comments about Wright's debt to Jones and Ruprich Robert can be found in James P. O'Gorman, *The Architecture of Frank Furness,* exhibition catalog (Philadelphia: Philadephia Museum of Art, 1973), 36–37.

11. I have consulted the revised edition (Cambridge: Cambridge University Press, 1948).

12. G. W. Sheldon, *Artistic Country-Seats: Types of Recent American Villa and Cottage Architecture with Instances of Country Club-Houses* (New York: D. Appleton, 1886), 1:61.

13. Spencer, "Wright," 64.

14. Donald Hoffmann, *The Architecture of John Wellborn Root* (Baltimore: Johns Hopkins University Press, 1973), 162.

15. Hugh Morrison, *Louis Sullivan: Prophet of Modern Architecture* (New York: Norton, 1962), pl. 31.

16. Albert Bush-Brown, *Louis Sullivan* (New York: George Braziller, 1960), fig. 42.

17. Alberto Izzo, Camillo Gubitosi, and Marcello Angrisani, *Frank Lloyd Wright disegni, 1887–1959* (Florence: Centro Di, 1976), fig. 2.

18. Grant Manson, *Frank Lloyd Wright to 1910: The First Golden Age* (New York: Van Nostrand Reinhold, 1958), 71–72, figs. 51–52.

19. William C. Gannett, Frank Lloyd Wright, and William Winslow, *The House Beautiful* (River Forest, Ill.: Auvergne Press, 1896–97); facsimile ed. (Park Forest, Ill.: W. R. Hasbrouck, 1963), unpaginated.

20. Henry-Russell Hitchcock, *The Architecture of H. H. Richardson and His Times,* rev. ed. (Cambridge, Mass.: MIT Press, 1966), 202–5.

21. Manson, *First Golden Age,* 75–76.

22. *Frank Lloyd Wright: Drawings from 1893–1959,* Exhibition and Sales for the Preservation of Taliesin, exhibition catalog from the Max Protetch Gallery, New York (Chicago: The Frank Lloyd Wright Foundation, 1983), 13–14.

23. Delivered March 6, 1901; reprinted in E. Kaufmann and B. Raeburn, eds., *Frank Lloyd Wright: Writings and Buildings* (New York: Horizon, 1960), 55–73. For bibliographical information see Robert Sweeney, *Frank Lloyd Wright: An Annotated Bibliography* (Los Angeles: Hennessey and Ingalls, 1978), 8–10.

24. David Hanks, *The Decorative Designs of Frank Lloyd Wright* (New York: E. P. Dutton, 1979), 39–41; and idem, "Frank Lloyd Wright's 'The Art and Craft of the Machine,'" in Kenneth Ames, ed., *Victorian Furniture: Essays from a Victorian Society Autumn Symposium,* vol. 8 of *The Nineteenth Century* (1982), 205–11.

25. Wright, "Art and Craft," 67; The Winslow Brothers Iron Company, *Collection of Photographs of Ornamental Iron* (Chicago, 1893).

26. See William Jordy, *Progressive and Academic Ideals at the Turn of the Twentieth Century,* vol. 3 of *American Buildings and Their Architects* (Garden City, N.Y.: Anchor Press, 1976), 88–100.

27. Wright, "Art and Craft," 67; *Catalogue of an Exhibition of the Etchings and Lithographs of James McNeill Whistler,* no. 3, *Nocturne.* (Chicago: The Caxton Club at the Art Institute, 1900), 39. See also Denys Sutton, *Nocturne: The Art of James McNeill Whistler* (London: Phaidon, 1983).

28. James McNeill Whistler, *Ten o'Clock Lecture* (1888); reprinted in Robert H. Getcher, *The Stamp of Whistler,* exhibition catalog, with an introduction by Allen Staley (Oberlin, Ohio: Allen Memorial Art Museum, 1977), 94.

29. Wright, "Art and Craft," 57. See also Wright, *Genius and the Mobocracy,* 12; and Wright, *An Autobiography,* 100.

Hugo quotations are from the translation of *Notre Dame de Paris* by J. Sturrock (Harmondsworth (England): Penguin Books, 1978), bk. 5, pp. 179–202.

On Hugo's knowledge of architecture, see Jean Mallion, *Victor Hugo et l'art architectural* (Paris: Presses Universitaires de France, 1962); and Neil Levine, "Architectural Reasoning in the Age of Positivism: The Neo-Grec Idea of Henri Labrouste's Bibliothèque Sainte-Geneviève," (Ph.D. diss., Yale University, 1975), 857–923, 1142 n. 1039.

30. Elizabeth Eisenstein, *The Printing Press as an Agent of Social Change,* 2 vols. (Cambridge: Cambridge University Press, 1979).

31. For the Corliss engine and its history see Robert C. Post, ed., *1876: A Centennial Exhibition* (Washington, D.C.: The Smithsonian Institution, 1976), 15, 29–33. By 1901 the engine had found its way to the Pullman car works, where Wright would have seen it: see Stanley Buder, *Pullman* (New York: Oxford University Press, 1976), 54.

32. Mark Reinberger, "The Sugarloaf Mountain Project and Frank Lloyd Wright's Vision of a New World," *Journal of the Society of Architectural Historians* 43 (1984): 38–52.

33. The romantic view of Wright is found in Fiske Kimball, *American Architecture* (Indianapolis: Bobbs-Merrill, 1928) 196 (from which the quotation is taken); and Henry-Russell Hitchcock, *Modern Architecture: Romanticism and Reintegration* (New York: Payson and Clarke, 1929), 115, 160, 212.

34. Norman Rice, "I Believe . . .," *T-Square* 2 (January 1932): 24–25, 34–35; Frank Lloyd Wright, "For All May Raise the Flowers Now, For All Have Got the Seed," *T-Square* 2 (February 1932): 6–8; George Howe, "Moses Turns Pharaoh," *T-Square* 2 (February 1932): 9; Frank Lloyd Wright, "Of Thee I Sing,"

Shelter 2 (April 1932) : 10–12. Other writings by Wright in the same vein are "Architecture as a Profession Is All Wrong," *The American Architect* 138 (December 1930) : 22–23ff; and "Caravel or Motorship," *Architectural Forum*, 57 (August 1932) : 90.

35. Buckminster Fuller, "Universal Architecture," *T-Square* 2 (February 1932) : 22ff.

36. Wright, "Of Thee I Sing," 10.

37. Frank Lloyd Wright, "Towards a New Architecture," *World Unity* 2 (September 1928) : 393–95. For Wright's influence on Le Corbusier, on the other hand, see Paul Venable Turner, "Frank Lloyd Wright and the Young Le Corbusier," *Journal of the Society of Architectural Historians* 42 (1983) : 350–59; 43 (1984) : 364–65.

38. Frank Lloyd Wright, *Modern Architecture, Being the Kahn Lectures for 1930* (Princeton: Princeton University Press, 1931); reprinted in Frank Lloyd Wright, *The Future of Architecture* (New York: Horizon Press, 1953), 107.

39. Wright, *Modern Architecture*, 65–80.

40. Donald Hoffman, *Frank Lloyd Wright's Fallingwater: The House and Its History* (New York: Dover, 1978), 16–17.

41. Henry-Russell Hitchcock and Philip Johnson, *The International Style: Architecture since 1922* (New York: Norton, 1932), 26: "Wagner, Behrens and Perret lightened the solid massiveness of traditional architecture; Wright dynamited it."

42. Joseph Connors, *The Robie House of Frank Lloyd Wright* (Chicago: University of Chicago Press, 1984), 40–45.

43. Letter of Frank Lloyd Wright to Harriet Monroe, 1907, quoted in Connors, *Robie House*, 69.

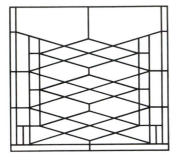

FRANK LLOYD WRIGHT'S OWN HOUSES AND HIS CHANGING CONCEPT OF REPRESENTATION

NEIL LEVINE

2

Despite the various new directions Wright scholarship has taken over the past two decades, the Prairie style he developed during the Oak Park years, culminating in the Robie house of 1908–09 (fig. 2.1), has remained until only very recently the central focus and defining term of most studies. Following the conventional historical account of modern architecture, dating from the late 1920s and early 1930s, Wright's realization of the Prairie House became the object toward which all his earlier work appeared to lead, and the *locus classicus* from which almost all his later work somehow diverged.[1] From the perspective of today, however—a perspective very different from that of fifty years ago—another, more comprehensive understanding of Wright's work seems called for. Ultimately, one will have to review and reconstruct the historical relation between his entire architectural production and the tradition of modernist architecture that began developing in Europe soon after the end of World War I. But, in order to do that, one will first have to reconsider the relation between Wright's earlier Prairie style and the architecture he produced during the fifty years following his departure from Oak Park in 1909. So, it is to the question of change and evolution in Wright's work prior to, but especially after, 1909 that this paper is addressed.

It is one of the commonplaces in the traditional narrative of modern architecture to refer to the significance of Wright's early work, or Prairie style, to explain the development of the International style in Europe in the late 1910s and 1920s.[2] Known primarily through the publications of the German Ernst Wasmuth in 1910 and 1911, buildings like the Robie house exerted a powerful influence on the younger European architects, such as Walter Gropius, Le Corbusier, and Mies van der Rohe, whose steel, concrete, and glass structures of the 1920s apparently showed the way in which Wright's fragmentation and decomposition of traditional form could be used to create an abstract architecture of lines and planes in space (fig. 2.2). But once Wright's Prairie style was defined and accepted as the catalytic agent in this development toward abstraction, Wright himself was relegated to the role of a forerunner. His Prairie style buildings were treated as the mature statement of his own art and little serious attention was paid to his work after 1910, which was generally felt to have represented a regression from the achievement of his earlier work. The later work was never really accepted as part of the canon of modern architecture and was seen as the personal, romantic, and totally idiosyncratic production of someone who followed only the whims of his own individual genius. Where the earlier work displayed a consistent pattern of planning and a rational use of materials that rigorously conformed to clearly established types, the later work seemed to disregard any discernable formula in the search for novelty and specificity of expression. If little connection was to be discerned between a building made out of desert boulders, redwood beams, and canvas tenting, such as Wright's own Taliesin West of 1938 and the nearly contemporary Guggenheim Museum, which looks like a smooth, industrialized ribbon of reinforced concrete, then obviously hardly any relation but the most meaningless and generalized sort of formal analogy could be drawn between such buildings as Taliesin West and the Robie house (figs. 2.32, 2.1).

What I shall propose, instead, is that there is a single intention that runs through all of Wright's work, connecting his earliest efforts to his last, and that essentially distinguishes his architecture from the modernist aesthetic of abstraction that emerged with the International style.[3] This was Wright's belief in architecture as an art of representation, in the classical meaning of that word as the imitation of nature.[4] The argument will be developed around a series of eight houses Wright designed for himself during his seventy-year career in which one can see the evolution of this controlling idea most completely expressed. In

2.1.   The Robie House, side
along 58th Street, looking
north. Courtesy Richard Nickel
committee.

2.2.   German Pavilion, International Exposition, Barcelona.
Ludwig Mies van der Rohe,
1928–29. Photograph courtesy
of Mies van der Rohe Archive,
The Museum of Modern Art,
New York.

these very personal designs, Wright was free to experiment as he wished. Of the eight houses, four were actually built, though only three remain. Of particular interest, moreover, is the fact that one of the unbuilt projects, and in this case the most crucial one, has only just recently been brought to light, never previously having been published nor even listed among Wright's projects.[5]

Wright himself never lived in a Prairie House, nor, as far as one can tell, did he ever design a typical one for his own use. His own houses show a concern for something quite different from the constant refinement of a type involved in the definition of the Prairie House. Beginning with the house he built for himself in Oak Park in 1889 (fig. 2.3), and ending with his final home in the Arizona desert of almost fifty years later, Wright's own houses explore the sources of symbolic expression in such a direct way as to exhibit more completely than any other group of buildings his changing concept of architecture as an art of representation. In time, Wright used his own houses as a kind of

2.3.   Frank Lloyd Wright house, Oak Park, Illinois. Frank Lloyd Wright, 1889. Photograph courtesy of The Museum of Modern Art, New York.

sketchbook, a record of his architectural response to nature and the surrounding landscape, so much so that buildings like Taliesin in Spring Green, Wisconsin, begun in 1911 (fig. 2.19), or the later Taliesin West, hardly seem like houses at all. Rather, they are like meditations on nature represented in the terms of architecture.

At the very beginning of Wright's career, things were obviously much less personalized and developed. Wright's house and studio in Oak Park, built at the time he began working for Louis Sullivan when he was just twenty-two years old, illustrates the first, most conventional stage in the evolution of his concept of architecture as the representation, or imitation, of nature. The exterior expression is reduced to the triangular shape of a gable set like a classical pediment above a supporting base of bay windows, while the interior is focused on a round-arched brick fireplace surrounded by an inglenook (figs. 2.3, 2.4). The exaggeration of these elements—the gable on the outside

2.4. Wright house, Oak Park. Living room, with fireplace. Photo by Donald G. Kalec, courtesy of the Frank Lloyd Wright Home and Studio Foundation, Oak Park.

and the arched fireplace on the inside—proclaims Wright's intention for the house to be read as the projection of an image of shelter, while the conventional shapes these symbols of hearth and home take reveal the representational basis of traditional architectural forms. Clearly, Wright was not being "original" in inventing these forms, as was shown long ago by Vincent Scully in noting Wright's dependence on the late Shingle style houses of Bruce Price, such as the Chandler house in Tuxedo Park of 1885–86 (fig. 2.5).[6] But the issue here is more than that of mere copying and has to do with the way the traditional forms of architecture were considered figures in a language based on the idea of representation.

Although we normally assume that architecture, unlike painting and sculpture, is an abstract art that makes no direct reference to nature, it can hardly be denied that the conventional shapes of traditional architecture stand in virtually the same relation to nature as the shapes of

2.5. W. Chandler house, Tuxedo Park, New York. Bruce Price, 1885–86. Reprinted from *Architecture* 1 (1900).

2.6. Frontispiece from Marc-Antoine Laugier, *Essay on Architecture,* second edition, 1755. From a drawing by Charles Eisen.

human figures in a painting do to the world of reality. Both depend on the acceptance of historical models in the process of imitation that Ernst Gombrich called the "making and matching" of art imitating art.[7] In architectural theory, it was, significantly enough, during the Enlightenment that the theory of imitation was applied to architecture in such a rational way as to affirm its representational basis. In his *Essay on Architecture* of 1753, the French theorist Marc-Antoine Laugier used the example of the primitive hut to testify to architecture's natural origins. He explained how the primitive hut was not merely the first example of built form, but the natural prototype for the conventional forms of classical architecture.[8] Imagining four trees growing out of the ground joined at the tops of their trunks by horizontal branches and supporting others set at an angle to one another, Laugier pictured in the celebrated frontispiece of the second edition (1755) of his book what he considered to be the most rational, and therefore natural, form of construction (fig. 2.6). He claimed that the Greeks first understood this and took the hut as the natural model for their temples. They transformed the various parts of the hut into stone, turning the tree trunks into columns, the horizontal branches into entablatures, and the angled branches into pediments. Thus, the Greek temple imitated in permanent materials the forms of nature and could therefore be considered the representation of the natural prototype of the hut. Once made permanent in stone, the conventional forms of the Greek temple became the ideal nature that all later architects would refer to and represent, just as the marble figures of Phidias or Praxiteles would form the images of ideal nature for the classical painter and sculptor.

Wright's classical project for the Milwaukee Public Library and Museum of 1893 (fig. 2.7) reveals that he too was fully conversant with this body of conventions and could, in fact, vary the mode of representation from the more rustic vernacular of his Oak Park house to the more idealized forms suitable for a public edifice.[9] Both these very early examples are representational buildings of a very conventional sort, using traditional forms to symbolize function through association.

It was the influence of Louis Sullivan, and especially the more abstract, typological thinking that resulted in his epoch-making Wainwright Building of 1890–91 (fig. 2.8) that allowed Wright in the Winslow

FRANK LLOYD WRIGHT'S OWN HOUSES

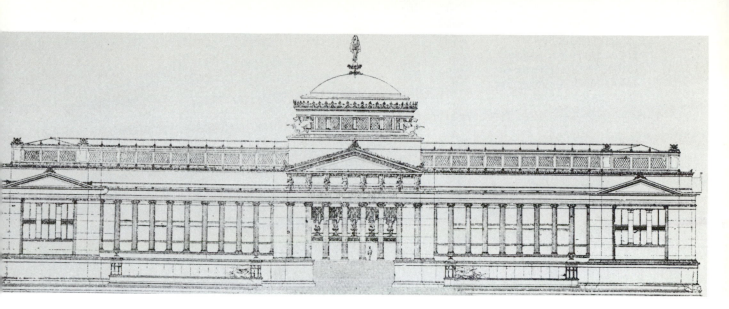

2.7. Frank Lloyd Wright project for Milwaukee Public Library and Museum, Milwaukee, Wisconsin, 1893. Elevation. Reprinted from Chicago Architectural Sketch Club, *Catalogue, Seventh Annual Exhibition,* May 1894.

house, of just two years later, to turn the conventional representation of shelter illustrated by his own Oak Park house into the more abstracted and stylized concept of the Prairie House (fig. 2.9).[10] Wright called the Winslow house "the first 'prairie house'" and considered it the original expression of the type.[11] The division of the house into a series of horizontal layers, beginning with a strong base and terminating in a deep decorative frieze under the broad overhanging plane of the roof, follows the pattern of Sullivan's typical division of the tall office building into its major functional units. As with Sullivan, the emphasis is taken off the associational references of conventional forms and is replaced by a more synthetic expression of programmatic meaning. In the Wainwright Building, the emotional sense of loftiness and power of commercial enterprise that Sullivan considered characteristic of the tall building is not expressed by the representation of a classical temple or Gothic tower, as it would have been in the ordinary skyscraper of the period. Rather, it is projected through the vertical lines of the structure itself, which are stylized, powerfully emphasized, and florescently climaxed in the cornice. Similarly, in the Winslow house, the elements of a house are now analyzed out into their constituent parts— entrance, ground-floor reception rooms, upper-floor bedrooms, roof,

and chimney. These are then synthesized into an image of domesticity that is not merely represented by any one or other conventional form, such as the gable or pediment, but is expressed in the emotional terms of horizontal lines that echo the earth and carry the sense of human warmth, comfort, and security—the opposite of Sullivan's aspiring and dominating image of commercial power, yet achieved by the same means of programmatic abstraction in terms of type.[12]

This delicate balance between convention and nature, between the general and the particular, between abstraction and representation,

FRANK LLOYD WRIGHT'S OWN HOUSES

2.9. Herman W. Winslow
house, River Forest, Illinois.
Frank Lloyd Wright, 1893. Photo
by author.

2.10. Edwin H. Cheney house,
Oak Park, Illinois. Frank Lloyd
Wright, 1904. Aerial perspec-
tive. Reprinted from Frank Lloyd
Wright, *Ausgeführte Bauten
und Entwürfe von Frank Lloyd
Wright,* 1910, pl. 30., by permis-
sion of the Houghton Library,
Harvard University.

became the key to the extraordinary tension that characterizes the
fully mature Prairie style that emerged during the following decade in
Wright's work and can be most movingly observed in the house he
built for Mamah and Edwin Cheney in Oak Park in 1904 (fig. 2.10).

FRANK LLOYD WRIGHT'S OWN HOUSES   29

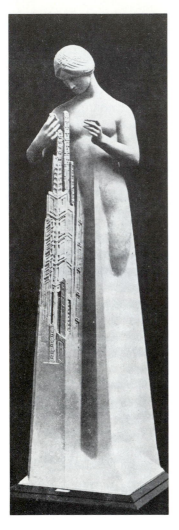

2.11. Frank Lloyd Wright and Richard W. Bock, *Flower in the Crannied Wall*, 1903–4. Susan L. Dana house, Springfield, Illinois, 1902–4. Reprinted from *Frank Lloyd Wright: Ausgeführte Bauten*, 1911.

Here, all the stylized elements of the Winslow house have been further abstracted and subjected to analysis. The house has been pulled apart, exploded as it were, into its constituent parts to allow each of the conventional elements—roof, wallplane, chimney, window band—to stand on its own without any direct connection to the traditional core, or mass, of the building still evident in the Winslow house. As the door frame of the Winslow house is pulled out to become the garden parapet wall of the Cheney house, and the roof plane of the Winslow house is made to float above the continuous window band of the Cheney house, the geometric shape and order of the elements come to dominate their representational character and thus force a much more complex reading than before. It is not that the traditional representational character of those elements is entirely given up but just that their degree of stylization is stretched to the limits. Wright was obviously aware of this duality or dichotomy as he seems to have made it the basis of the sculptural image of architecture he designed just a year or so before to stand in the entrance hall of the Dana house in Springfield, Illinois (fig. 2.11).

The *Flower in the Crannied Wall*, as the sculpture executed by his associate Richard Bock was entitled, shows a female muse of architecture, like the one pointing to the primitive hut in Laugier's frontispiece, building herself a crystalline tower out of geometric blocks.[13] The completely abstract design of the tower is contrasted with the quite sensuous representation of a woman, but both tower and woman are seen to be emerging from the same block of brute matter or stone. As a result, we do not simply read the image of architecture as an abstraction, but rather in the dialectical terms of nature and geometry working together to produce a composition of conventionalized, or stylized, forms grounded in the world of representation and taking its order from that creative impulse. In the sculpture of the *Flower in the Crannied Wall*, then, abstraction and representation are seen to be in balance, as the conventionalized forms of architecture emerge out of the process, and through the medium, of representation.

Maintaining this balance between two such extremes, fundamentally opposed in their purposes, seems to have remained Wright's ideal for the rest of the decade. It also seems, however, that the growing

FRANK LLOYD WRIGHT'S OWN HOUSES

2.12. (Right) Frank Lloyd Wright, project for his own studio-house, Oak Park, Illinois, c. 1903–4. Plan. (Left) Cheney house plan. Reprinted from Wright, *Ausgeführte Bauten und Entwürfe*, pl. 30., by permission of the Houghton Library, Harvard University.

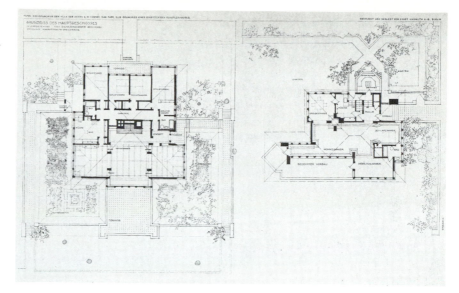

domination of the extreme of abstraction, which appears so forcefully in buildings like the Robie house (fig. 2.1), led Wright to question the direction of his work at that point and to put an end, in his words, to this "phase of [his] experience as an architect."[14] Certainly, personal factors were involved, but it is abundantly clear from what he said that Wright believed his architecture was "up against a dead wall"—at the end of a "closed road."[15] And so, at just about the time the Robie house was being completed, Wright left his Oak Park home, family, and practice for good and eloped to Europe for a year with Mamah Cheney, the wife of his former client. In the Wasmuth portfolio he produced while living in Florence during that year, Wright illustrated in a most curious yet revealing way the only other house design he is known to have done for himself before 1909. It is shown in plan only on the same sheet as the plan of the Cheney house (fig. 2.12).[16] Though simply identified as an artist's house on the plate, and not even referred to in the accompanying legend, this design of about 1903–4 was apparently made by Wright as a single-story, open-plan studio-house for himself. Or was it in fact to be shared with someone else?[17] That might explain why he paired it with the Cheney house. But clearly, Wright also

2.13. Villa Medici, Fiesole, Italy. Michelozzo, 1458–61. View from southeast. Photo: Alinari/Art Resource, New York.

meant to compare its completely atypical, asymmetrical, and particularized design with the symmetrical, abstractly ordered Cheney house to contrast the ideas an artist can develop for himself with what he must do to respond to the needs of a client. Since we have no elevation of Wright's studio-house of 1903–4, it is hard to say much more, except to reiterate that, even in the high moment of his creation of the Prairie House, Wright chose not to see himself in its typical forms.

Wright's desire to break the type, to break the mold, in order to regain a greater degree of naturalism and freedom from the abstract order of convention, which was already evident in the second house he designed for himself, was what led him, oddly enough, to spend the year abroad not in Berlin, the hotbed of developing modernism, but in and around Florence, a place where to some architecture surely seemed to have stopped with the Renaissance.[18] But for Wright, the villas and gardens in the surrounding hilltowns such as Fiesole, where he eventually chose to rent a small *villino* with a garden overlooking the "romantic city of Cities,"[19] brought architecture and nature together in such a remarkable union that it satisfied his need to experience a world

FRANK LLOYD WRIGHT'S OWN HOUSES

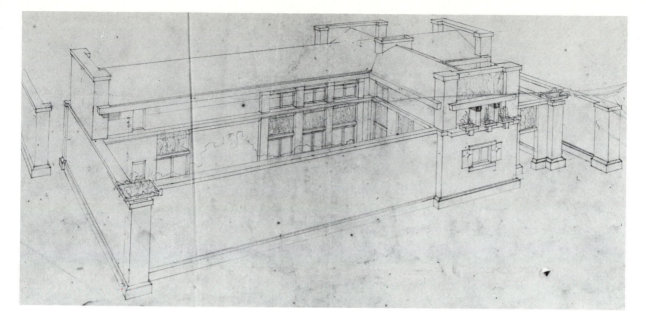

2.14. Frank Lloyd Wright, project for his own house, Fiesole, 1910. Aerial perspective. Courtesy of The Frank Lloyd Wright Memorial Foundation.

in which the classical idea of the imitation of nature could be understood all over again (fig. 2.13).

Italy revealed its lesson very slowly to Wright. It only just begins to make itself felt in the house Wright designed for himself and Mamah Cheney in 1910 for a hillside site in Fiesole not far from Michelozzo's Villa Medici (fig. 2.14).[20] In this project, Wright formalized the Prairie House type not in terms of greater abstraction but rather in terms of classical ordonnance and site planning. The gridded facades, filled in with relief panels of sculpture, rise above the low rooflines and mark the boundaries of secret gardens, enclosed, like those of the surrounding Italian villas, by high blank walls. There is little of the typical Prairie House's sense of extension into the landscape by means of overhanging eaves and open porches, and yet there is much more real interaction with the hillside site through the characteristic use of walled gardens to produce an effect so similar to the terracing of the Villa Medici.

In 1911, soon after he returned to the United States, Wright designed two more houses for himself, showing the two different sides of

2.15.   Frank Lloyd Wright, project for his own house, Goethe Street, Chicago, 1911. Perspective. Courtesy of The Frank Lloyd Wright Memorial Foundation.

what he learned in Italy. In the townhouse he intended to be built on Goethe Street on the near north side of Chicago, just a few blocks from Cedar Street where he was renting a place, Wright adapted the classicizing facade of his projected Fiesole villa to the formal, urban context of a downtown street (fig. 2.15).[21] But in the country estate he began building in Wisconsin in the summer of that year, on the land that his Welsh forefathers had settled in the previous century, Wright found the liberation from convention that he had been searching for. He developed, out of his experience of the classical Italian villa and garden, a new and completely original interpretation of architecture as the *direct* imitation of nature (fig. 2.16).[22]

Wright named the house Taliesin, which means "shining brow" in Welsh, and designed it as a series of wings forming a loosely C-shaped court following the contours of the hill and set just below its crown. Above a formal hillside garden, the hilltop, with its grove of oak trees, is bordered by a semicircular stone exedra (fig. 2.17). All the materials—the stone, the wood, and the sand for the plaster—are local and are used with a feeling for their natural properties that is quite different from the way in which Wright had previously designed for the suburbs and city of Chicago.[23] As if to illustrate in the most explicit way the difference between Taliesin and the earlier Prairie House type, Wright used a second cast of the sculpture of the *Flower in the Crannied Wall* from the Dana house to define the pivotal spot of his hillside dwelling. Instead of appearing, as in the Dana house, framed by an arch built of Roman brick and cut stone on the central axis of the entrance hall (fig. 2.18), the figure at Taliesin is placed out in the open at the edge of the drive up against the hillslope (fig. 2.19). In the Dana house, it appears as a chink of light through the door, highlighting by its shape and color the conventional representation of the entrance way. Indeed, its image there of abstract form growing out of the ground of representation almost seems to describe the very design of the house itself—a conventional representation stylized to the point where historical form becomes hardly more than a dim memory (fig. 2.20).

In Taliesin, by contrast, the sculptured figure appears to grow out of the hillside, like the surrounding trees and shrubs and stone walls. It no longer points to a distinction between geometry and nature, or

2.16.   Taliesin, Spring Green, Wisconsin. Frank Lloyd Wright, begun 1911. General view from south. Photo courtesy of Hedrich-Blessing, Chicago.

2.17.   Taliesin. Hill-garden and court, looking southeast toward living quarters. Reprinted from H. Th. Wijdeveld, ed., *The Life-Work of the American Architect Frank Lloyd Wright (Wendingen)*, 1925.

2.18. Susan L. Dana house, Springfield, Illinois. Frank Lloyd Wright, 1902–4. Entrance. Reprinted from *Frank Lloyd Wright, Ausgeführte Bauten,* 1911.

abstraction and representation, but rather signifies a continuity or identity of the two. In Taliesin, the *Flower in the Crannied Wall* occupies the point where nature and architecture come together—the juncture of the natural and the man-made—with the hillside rising "unbroken" and undisturbed above it,[24] and the house growing out of it like a ledge beneath it.

Wright described Taliesin as the first "natural house," and believed he had achieved an equivalence for nature in its architecture.[25] Although the actual forms of the hip roofs, freestanding piers, and paneled planes remind us of his earlier work, Wright transcended the conventional model of representation by reworking these forms so as to imitate, now *directly,* the very appearance of nature. In his *Autobiography,* he explained:

FRANK LLOYD WRIGHT'S OWN HOUSES

2.19.   Taliesin. Hill-garden with *Flower in the Crannied Wall*. Photograph courtesy of The Frank Lloyd Wright Memorial Foundation.

2.20.   Dana house. Photo courtesy of Budek Films and Slides, Newport, R.I.

Taliesin was to be a combination of stone and wood as they met in the aspect of the hills around about [fig. 2.21]. The lines of the hills were the lines of the roofs. The slopes of the hills their slopes, the plastered surfaces of the light wood-walls, set back into shade beneath broad eaves, were like the flat stretches of sand in the river below and the same in color, for that is where the material that covered them came from.

The finished wood outside was the color of gray tree-trunks, in violet light.

The shingles of the roof surfaces were left to weather, silver-gray like the tree branches spreading below them. (P. 174)

Wright wanted his house in Wisconsin literally to look like part of the hillside, to "belong to that hill, as trees and the ledges of rock did," so that one could hardly tell "where pavements and walls left off and the ground began" (pp. 171, 173). He said he "scanned the hills of the region where the rock came cropping out in strata to suggest build-

FRANK LLOYD WRIGHT'S OWN HOUSES

2.22. Taliesin. General view from northeast. Photo courtesy of Sandak, Inc., Stamford, Connecticut.

ings" and took the image of these rock outcrops as the model for the stonework of the house (p. 171). He directed the masons to imitate the "pattern" of rough ledges, or strata, of rock as they were "exposed" in the quarry located just over the next hill (pp. 174, 173). In this way, Wright sought to make Taliesin give the appearance of a natural outcropping and thus become what the word Taliesin meant—the "shining brow" of the hill (fig. 2.22). With the hill crown rising within and above it, house and hill would then "live together each the happier for the other," as Wright said. Such "a house that hill might marry and live happily with ever after," in perfect natural union, would thus express the same hope Wright held out for his relationship with Mamah Cheney, "she for whom Taliesin had first taken form" (p. 189).

That ideal union, however, was shattered by the multiple murders and fire at Taliesin in the summer of 1914. Wright's cook went mad, setting fire to the house when Wright was away and then hacking to death Mamah Cheney, her two children, plus four employees, and thereby destroying, it would seem forever, Wright's naive belief in the possibility of a completely natural and direct identification of architecture and nature. Most of the next seven or eight years were spent far away from his home, working on the Imperial Hotel in Tokyo (1916–22) where, instead of imagining an architecture at one with a benevolent landscape, Wright now saw the process of building as a confrontation with the violent and irrational forces of nature embodied in volcanos and earthquakes.[26] "Building against doomsday," as he later put it,[27] Wright returned, almost with a vengeance, to the historical forms and patterns of conventional representation. The Imperial Hotel, like the contemporary Hollyhock house (1919–21), was laid out on a symmetrical, hierarchically organized plan and articulated three-dimensionally in elaborate, decorative dress.

It is against this background of displacement and sublimation that we must see the design of the sixth house Wright planned for himself, the one which, for whatever reason, he chose never to make public. Two autograph drawings for it exist, a plan and a side elevation (figs. 2.23, 2.24).[28] They were apparently done, while Wright was in Southern California, for a site in the Mojave Desert, most probably in or near Death Valley. Bruce Brooks Pfeiffer, the Director of Archives of the Frank Lloyd Wright Memorial Foundation, has very convincingly suggested that this project may be connected with the commission for the wealthy Chicago insurance man Albert M. Johnson's ranch in Death Valley, on the site of what is now Scotty's Castle. This would mean that the design dates from somewhere between 1921 and 1923–24.[29] It is extraordinary and reveals a complete change in Wright's concept of representation. Planned for the vast expanse of the desert, it is the first of Wright's buildings after the Taliesin fire to suggest that, by turning to an entirely new model of imitation, Wright could continue to develop the promise of a natural architecture held out by Taliesin. The compact, two-story house is clearly as symbolic and as imagistic in intention as was Wright's original Oak Park house and studio. The actual living section of the small building is tucked onto the rear of an octagonal court, entered on axis and open to the sky.[30] The walls of the octagon open out like the petals of a desert flower to hold in tension an overhead awning. A central oculus is situated directly above a circular pool, cut into the desert floor just in front of a monumental

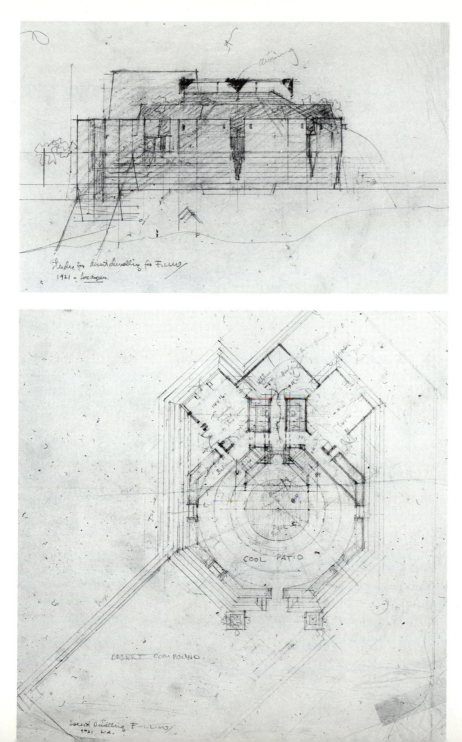

2.23. Frank Lloyd Wright, project for his own "Desert Dwelling," Death Valley, Mojave Desert (?), California, c. 1921–24. Elevation. Courtesy of The Frank Lloyd Wright Memorial Foundation.

2.24. Wright, project for his own "Desert Dwelling," plan. Courtesy of The Frank Lloyd Wright Memorial Foundation.

chimney that divides into two the stairways leading to balconies and the rooms behind.

At first glance the house has the appearance of a barbican, obviously defensive in nature.[31] But soon that image dissolves into something more like a cistern or vessel, protected from, yet receptive to the elements. The defensive, inward-looking *parti* of a courtyard dwelling immediately reminds us of Hollyhock house, which Wright had just completed in Los Angeles in 1921. There, a central courtyard, open to the sky, contains a stream of water connecting reflecting pools at each end of the house (fig. 2.25). But the forms of Hollyhock house, as well as its materials of construction, are quite different. The sham wood and stucco walls and canted roofs imitate the shapes of Maya temples in an unusually direct, historicizing way. In Wright's project for a "desert dwelling," on the other hand, the forms are treated in such a plastic manner as to suggest the use of reinforced concrete and probably, in fact, Wright's new method of textile-block construction. But, more important, they make no reference to any historical type of architecture and rather seem to grow out of the ground in an entirely unpredictable, yet natural, way.

FRANK LLOYD WRIGHT'S OWN HOUSES

2.26. Taliesin. Pool in entrance court with Ming jar. Photo by E. Teske. First published in *Architectural Forum* 68 (January 1938).

The image of a cistern or pot, which is indeed the underlying image suggested by this project, was one that was particularly in evidence in Wright's thinking at the time. During the years Wright was in Japan, he collected many, many works of Oriental art, the most striking of which were the various vessels, and particularly the Tea Jars, he then incorporated into the reconstruction of Taliesin (fig. 2.26). He placed them on the ledges and parapets of his house, as if to signify some new meaning he was trying to return to those walls embracing the hill crown he described soon after the fire as the "smoking crater of a volcano."[32] The idea of the fired vessel or pot became for Wright an image of regeneration, and its shape, totally continuous and protective yet wholly responsive to its contents, presented a new model for representation. Unlike the classical archetype of the hut, the vessel or pot was plastic rather than clastic, spatial rather than structural.[33] Unlike other archetypal models, such as the cave or the tent, the pot provided a continuous image of inside and outside at once, while remaining stable and permanent in shape.[34] The earthenware vessel or pot was, by its very nature, *of* the earth, a realization in three-dimensional form of the holes in the ground that may have served as the basis for the pit-houses of the

2.27. Panamint basket, Great Basin, California, early twentieth century. Photo by Carmelo Guadagno, courtesy of Museum of the American Indian, Heye Foundation, New York.

prehistoric American Indians, some of the earliest known dwellings of the region of the Southwest Wright had chosen to build in.

Indeed, if the first pots Wright prized came from the Orient, it was the experience of the American Southwest and its Indian culture that gave Wright a historical rationale for such a model that can surely stand up to Laugier's defense of the hut.[35] In the Mojave Desert, and in particular Death Valley, Wright would have seen the baskets woven by the Panamint Indians and collected by Albert Johnson's wife Bessie that were thought to have preceded the more permanent fired clay vessels of the later Pueblo cultures (fig. 2.27).[36] These surely suggested to him both the decorative patterns of the forms of his desert dwelling as well as the textile-block method of construction he would no doubt have used to build it, but even beyond that, the *sequence* of transformations from one material to another that might lead from the impermanent to the permanent—from portable container to architecture.[37]

In his only essay treating the history of architectural development, a part of which was published in the following decade, Wright described how man, who "probably first lived in stone caves, when he did not live in trees," soon learned a new method for shaping the structures around him subsequent to his change from basketmaking to the production of pottery:[38]

> While still dwelling in caves . . . man perhaps learned to make utensils out of wet clay. He burned them hard for use. These utensils he seems to have made with a higher faculty. His instinct became an aesthetic sense of environment. It taught him something of form. He learned from the animals, the serpents, the plants that he knew. Except for this faculty he was no more than another animal.
>
> Still clinging to the cliffs, he made whole caves out of wet clay and let the sun bake the cave hard. He made them just as he had made the vessels that he had previously put into the fire to bake and had used in the cave in the rocks. And so, once upon a time, man moved into his first earth-built house, of *earth*.
>
> This large clay cave or pot of the cliff-dwellers, with a lid on it, was among the first man-made houses. The lid was troublesome to him then and has always been so to subsequent builders.[39]

FRANK LLOYD WRIGHT'S OWN HOUSES

2.28. Cliff Palace, Mesa Verde, Colorado, thirteenth century. Photo by author.

If the kivas in such cliff-dwellings as those in Mesa Verde (fig. 2.28) represented the original form of the storage pot or cistern and thereby derived their sacred meaning from that transformation, as suggested by Alfred Kidder in his classic *Introduction to the Study of Southwestern Archaeology* of 1924,[40] then the even earlier version of the woven basket carried the image of the protective vessel of space back to a pre-lithic, truly hut-like condition, providing a mythic dimension to Wright's theory to match Laugier's own. Ignoring the fact that the cliff-dwellings he had in mind were constructed of coursed stone rather than molded out of clay, Wright was able to imagine a perfectly consistent historical evolution of form. And, this revelation of a different, more plastic model of imitation gave Wright a new basis for representation that wholly redirected his thinking about architecture.

From the mid-1920s on, and only from that time on, did Wright begin speaking of his buildings as vessels of space and of his architecture as an "architecture of the *within*."[41] It was apparently then that he first read Okakura's *Book of Tea* and discovered in its pages the words of Lao-tse describing the "'reality of the building'" as "'the space within to be

FRANK LLOYD WRIGHT'S OWN HOUSES

2.29.   Ocatilla, near Chandler,
Arizona. Frank Lloyd Wright,
1929. General view. Photograph
courtesy of The Frank Lloyd
Wright Memorial Foundation.

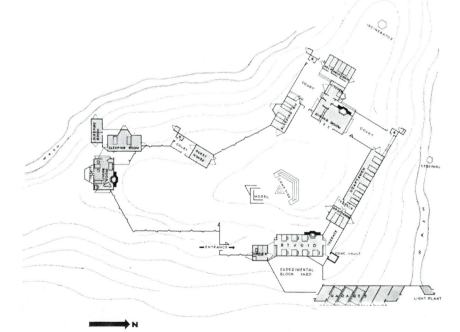

2.30.   Ocatilla plan. Reprinted
from *Architectural Record* 68
(August 1930). Courtesy of Architectural Record.

"OCATILLA"   N   DESERT CAMP FOR FRANK LLOYD WRIGHT, ARIZONA

lived in.'"[42] From these he extrapolated back to reinterpret the meaning
of his earlier buildings such as Unity Temple.[43] From the point of view of
representation, however, the change was perhaps even greater, for this
new model released Wright from almost all ties to traditional structural
conventions and allowed him to pursue with singlemindedness the
more direct imitation of natural appearances first achieved in Taliesin.
Finally, the evolutionary implication of transformation from a less permanent and portable object to a more stable, monumental form of
building brought to Wright's method of representation a historical dimension that would ultimately channel his work in a completely logical,
though entirely unexpected, direction.

   Wright's final two dwellings, both designed for the area around
Phoenix, Arizona, develop in a fully realized way all the implications of
his original desert project. Ocatilla was built at the foot of the South
(Salt River) Mountains in January 1929 to serve as a temporary camp for
however many seasons it would take Wright to construct the luxury
San Marcos-in-the-Desert Hotel.[44] More than a dozen individual units
of wood and canvas were joined together by a girding box-board wall
that zigzagged in and out along the contours of the oblong mound to

form a "compound" in Wright's words (figs. 2.29, 2.30).[45] The containing wall was painted a rose color to imitate the light on the desert floor, while the 30°–60° triangles at the ends of the canvas roofs were painted scarlet to look like the small red flowers of the spindly ocotillo cactus for which the camp was named. While the angles of the roofs were meant to echo the shapes of the surrounding mountains, and the zigzagging walls containing and protecting the interior space recalled the movement of the rattlesnakes and sidewinders they were intended to keep out, the general effect of light, flapping canvas above earth-colored walls represented in Wright's eyes both the image of butterfly wings fluttering above land and the sails of some new form of desert ship or vessel moving through space.[46] Each unit was treated like an individual vessel of space (fig. 2.31). Modeled on the idea of a container, each was surrounded on four sides by the box-board wall and had for its lid a luminous canvas topping. This allowed the sun to penetrate only from above and to give to each part of the compound, as to the whole, a sense of being contained within the circle of the sun's life-giving rays.

Taliesin West, the permanent desert camp Wright finally built some nine years later to the east of Phoenix, on Maricopa Mesa below the McDowell Mountains, made the angled forms he chose for Ocatilla solid and monumental in concrete and stone, while retaining the wood and canvas roofs to preserve the model of the building as lidded pot (fig. 2.32).[47] Taliesin West is, perhaps more than any other built work of Wright's, explicitly pot-like, appearing at times like a group of ancient pots lying upright on the mesa floor.[48] Wright used unlidded portions of the structure to contain plants and flowers. In the focal corner of the living room of his domestic quarters, Wright hollowed out a small, well-like garden court (fig. 2.33). Within its glass enclosure, right opposite the entrance to the room, he framed and displayed, as if floating miraculously in space, two Han dynasty funerary urns, which thus dramatize and, as it were, materialize the underlying image of the vessel or pot. They are like prehistoric relics, unearthed and newly brought to light.

If the angled forms of the stone walls of Taliesin West remind us of the shape of a pot's neck, the grooved lines etched in the concrete call

FRANK LLOYD WRIGHT'S OWN HOUSES

2.32. Taliesin West, Scottsdale, Arizona. Frank Lloyd Wright, begun 1938. Entrance court looking toward Wright's office-study. Photo by author.

2.33. Taliesin West. Living-room interior. Photograph courtesy of The Frank Lloyd Wright Memorial Foundation.

to mind the streamlines of erosion one sees in the nearby canyons, thus giving the impression that one is not only looking at the outside of an architectural container but that one is actually inside seeing the effect of wind and water wearing away the interior walls (fig. 2.34). That sense of natural action over time is reinforced by the appearance, at the main entrance, of an ancient Indian petroglyph boulder (fig. 2.35). While it marks the axis of approach to the drafting room and living quarters, it also signifies that the site may just fit into a larger historical time frame than one first expected. This boulder, along with other similar ones Wright found in the area, clearly indicated the existence of an earlier, prehistoric occupation of the site, and Wright's reuse of such remains in his design established a continuity with that past.[49]

The camp, in its desert environment, seems more like the archeo-logical remains of an ancient civilization than a new building. Wright's last wife, Olgivanna, always said Taliesin West looked more like some-thing being excavated than something being constructed.[50] This quality of appearing like a site strewn with potsherds and low rubble walls, now covered over in part to contain some new use, is driven home by

2.35. Taliesin West. Entrance with petroglyph boulder. Photo by author.

the petroglyph boulders located at two crucial places. The first one, as we have seen (fig. 2.35), is isolated on the prow at the entrance to the precinct and framed by the buildings around it, for which it serves as a point of orientation. The second one, which Wright placed on a high pyramidal base above a pool in front of the drafting room, is contained within the triangular terrace of the camp and marks the axis of orientation to the mountains beyond (fig. 2.36). In contrast to the actual forms of the building, which imitate the lines and colors and textures of the surrounding landscape in order to appear as a natural outgrowth of it, the petroglyph boulders, with their ancient, cryptic messages, give a temporal dimension to the site and make the present building seem to share a history with nature.[51] Nature, as an object of representation, therefore becomes inseparable from its historical manifestations, and the power of the model to contain that series of transformations is forcefully reaffirmed in purely twentieth-century terms.

In Taliesin West, the final house he built for himself, Wright thus reintroduced, in the most personal of ways, that historical framework which had always supported the classical theory of imitation; and it

2.36.   Taliesin West. View north from terrace toward McDowell Mountains, with petroglyph boulder above pool. Photo by author.

was this final revision of representation that dominated his thinking over the last two decades of his career. From the later 1930s on, he began using the circle, both as a two-dimensional element in plan and a three-dimensional form in space, to embody in the most direct way possible the model of representation he had evolved. At first, the imagery of these designs was generally related to the abstract idea of water.[52] But then, in buildings such as the Guggenheim Museum, designed just after Taliesin West was finished though only built a decade later, and the Marin County Civic Center in California, built at the same time as the Guggenheim in the late 1950s, Wright took as his starting point the architectural vessel or container but also gave a historical shape to the buildings' natural imagery. The great vessel of the Guggenheim, which joins the light from above to a pool of water at its base (fig. 2.37), just as Wright's project for his own house in the desert did thirty years before, spirals out in the form of a Babylonian ziggurat to give the visitor the feeling of being suspended in time, in a fluid

FRANK LLOYD WRIGHT'S OWN HOUSES

2.37.   Interior view of Solomon R. Guggenheim Museum, New York. Frank Lloyd Wright, 1943–59. Photo by Robert E. Mates, courtesy of The Solomon R. Guggenheim Museum.

2.38.   Marin County Civic Center, Santa Venetia, California. Frank Lloyd Wright, 1957–70. Interior. Photo by author.

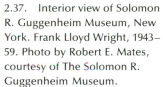

2.39. Marin County Civic Center. View from Hall of Justice, looking south. Photo by author.

environment that would appear, Wright hoped, to be like a "still wave, never breaking, never offering resistance or finality to vision."[53]

In the Marin County Civic Center, designed in 1957, Wright stretched the connection between history and nature as far as he ever would, treating the vessel of the Guggenheim as if it were purely plastic (fig. 2.38), pulling it out into the shape of a Roman aqueduct, like the famous Pont du Gard, near Nîmes (fig. 2.39). But the long, V-shaped building does not simply represent a Roman structure. Rather, it goes beyond the form itself and represents, through that type of vessel, the actual transformation of nature for the public good by the imitation of the movement of water. Located at the base of the Coastal Range of mountains separating the San Francisco and San Pablo bays from the Pacific Ocean, the building projects north from the direction of Mt. Tamalpais and seems, with its aqua-blue roof emerging from the hillside, literally to draw the water out of the rock and conduct it along a course that apparently follows the direction of an underground stream, and, to deposit the water, before angling west 40°, in a man-made lake that is ultimately channeled around and out into the bay (fig. 2.40).

FRANK LLOYD WRIGHT'S OWN HOUSES

2.40. Marin County Civic Center. General view southwest from lake. Photo by author.

At first glance, nothing might appear further removed from that direct imitation of nature that Wright first achieved in Taliesin (see fig. 2.21) than the Marin County Civic Center of almost half a century later. But Wright himself never believed there was a break in his work after 1910. He attempted throughout his career, and up until the very end, to emphasize the continuity of intention I have tried to outline. One of the last things he did, in fact, toward the very end of his life, was to dramatize, at Taliesin itself, the model of the vessel or earthenware pot that he had turned to in the early 1920s as the means for regenerating his art. Sometime after the fire of 1914, when he clearly gave up any hope of reviving his earlier practice and the traditional concept of representation embodied in the Prairie style, Wright removed the sculpture of the *Flower in the Crannied Wall,* which had symbolized that ambition, from its prominent location on the hillslope and eventually placed it underground, at the entrance to the root cellar. In return, and by way of contrast, he crowned the crest of the hill, that part of the natural landscape he had so poignantly left untouched in 1911, with an enormous Ming tub, aqua-blue like the roof of the

FRANK LLOYD WRIGHT'S OWN HOUSES

Marin County Civic Center, like the water its shape was made to contain (fig. 2.41).[54]

After seeing the idea of making that perfect representation of nature, that Taliesin once was, destroyed and turned into the "smoking crater of a volcano," it is as if the great pot on the hillcrown above Taliesin was put there by Wright to acknowledge that, in the end, it is naive for any artist to believe he can engage nature directly and form an image of it on his own each time. But if he wants to carry on that monumental tradition of representational architecture, he must have a model that connects his vision of nature to history, one that is integral to his culture and derives its meaning from that connection. For Wright, as I hope to have shown, it was the earthenware pot he embodied first in his own house for the Mojave Desert that furnished this key to the rest of his work. That model allowed him to ground his revolutionary idea of architecture as space in an ever-expanding series of references to nature and to history, and that gave renewed life in the twentieth century to the classical tradition of architecture as an art of representation.

FRANK LLOYD WRIGHT'S OWN HOUSES

NOTES

This paper was originally delivered as a talk in the Robie House Symposium held at the University of Chicago in October 1984. I am extremely grateful to the Frank Lloyd Wright Memorial Foundation and, in particular, to its Director of Archives, Bruce Brooks Pfeiffer, for the generous help they provided. The research for this study was supported, in part, by a fellowship from the Graham Foundation for Advanced Studies in the Fine Arts.

1. For the main outlines of this account, see the following sequence of articles and books: Henry-Russell Hitchcock, "Modern Architecture," *Architectural Record* 63 (April–May 1928), pt. 1 ("The Traditionalists and the New Tradition"): 337–49; pt. 2 ("The New Pioneers"): 453–60; Henry-Russell Hitchcock, *Modern Architecture: Romanticism and Reintegration* (New York: Payson and Clarke, 1929); Henry-Russell Hitchcock and Philip Johnson, *The International Style: Architecture since 1922* (New York: W. W. Norton & Company, 1932).

2. For discussions of Wright's influence on and relation to European modernism, see, for example, Nikolaus Pevsner, "Frank Lloyd Wright's Peaceful Penetration of Europe," *Architects' Journal* 89 (4 May 1939): 731–34; Henry-Russell Hitchcock, "Wright's Influence Abroad," *Parnassus* 12 (December 1940): 11–15; Vincent Scully, "Wright vs. the International Style," *Art News* 53 (March 1954): 32–35, 64–66; Edgar Kaufmann, Jr., "Frank Lloyd Wright's Years of Modernism, 1925–1935," *Journal of the Society of Architectural Historians* 25 (March 1965): 31–33; Heidemarie Kief, *Der Einfluss Frank Lloyd Wrights auf die Mitteleuropäische Einzelhausarchitektur: Ein Beitrag zum Verhältnis von Architektur und Natur in 20. Jahrhundert* (Stuttgart: Karl Krämer, 1978); and Paul Venable Turner, "Frank Lloyd Wright and the Young Le Corbusier," *Journal of the Society of Architectural Historians* 42 (December 1983): 350–59.

3. For a somewhat different treatment of this same issue, see Neil Levine, "Abstraction and Representation in Modern Architecture: Frank Lloyd Wright and the International Style," *AA Files: Annals of the Architectural Association School of Architecture* 11 (Spring 1986): 3–21.

4. For his most cogent expression of a Platonic theory of imitation, see Frank Lloyd Wright, *The Japanese Print: An Interpretation* (1912; New York, Horizon Press, 1967).

5. The houses to be discussed here are: house and studio, Oak Park, Illinois, 1889; studio-house project, Oak Park, c. 1903–4; house project, Fiesole, Italy, 1910; Goethe Street townhouse project, Chicago, 1911; Taliesin, Spring Green, Wisconsin, begun 1911; desert house project, Death Valley (?), Mojave Desert, California, c. 1921–24; Ocatilla, near Chandler, Arizona, 1929; Taliesin

West, Scottsdale, Arizona, begun 1938. The number eight is in no way meant to be definitive since, as in the case of the desert house project, a previously unpublished design may still turn up. For reasons of consistency of program and type, I am restricting myself to complete buildings and therefore will not discuss remodelings, such as the suite Wright redecorated for his own use in the Plaza Hotel in New York in the 1950s, or sections of larger buildings, such as the apartment in the Imperial Hotel in Tokyo which Wright designed for himself in 1920. I shall be considering both Taliesin and Taliesin West in terms of their initial designs and campaigns of construction, rather than as ongoing projects. In this regard I will not discuss any remodeling of an earlier structure, such as the later additions or changes to the Oak Park house and studio. Nor will I refer to any reprise or recycling of an earlier structure, such as the apparent removal of parts of Ocatilla to the Indiana Dunes, as reported by a Belgian visitor to the United States in 1930. J. Moutschen, "Souvenirs sur Frank Lloyd Wright," *La Cité et Tekhné* 10 (November 1931): 41–43.

6. Vincent Scully, *The Shingle Style: Architectural Theory and Design from Richardson to the Origins of Wright* (New Haven: Yale University Press, 1955), 159. As Scully points out, the Chandler house was published in *Building: A Journal of Architecture* 5 (18 September 1886). A number of Bruce Price's houses were also published in George W. Sheldon, *Artistic Country Seats,* 2 vols. (New York, 1886–87). Wright himself seems to have been quite conscious of such sources, later recalling that people passing by his "funny little house . . . used to ask me if it were Seaside or Colonial." Frank Lloyd Wright, *Genius and the Mobocracy* (New York: Duell, Sloan and Pearce, 1949), 42.

7. Ernst Gombrich, *Art and Illusion: A Study in the Psychology of Pictorial Representation,* The A. W. Mellon Lectures in the Fine Arts, 1956, Bollingen Series 35, vol. 5, 2d ed., rev. (New York: Bollingen Foundation/Pantheon Books, 1961).

8. For the most recent translation and presentation, see Marc-Antoine Laugier, *An Essay on Architecture,* trans. and with an Introduction by Wolfgang and Anni Herrmann, vol. 1 of *Documents and Sources in Modern Architecture* (Los Angeles: Hennessey & Ingalls, 1977).

9. The competition for the combined library and museum was held in 1893. Although Wright's design was not premiated, it was shown in the annual exhibition of the Chicago Architectural Sketch Club of May 1894 and reproduced in the accompanying catalog. For an early study of Wright's relation to the classical tradition, see Henry-Russell Hitchcock, "Frank Lloyd Wright and the 'Academic Tradition' of the Early Eighteen-Nineties," *Journal of the Warburg and Courtauld Institutes* 7 (1944): 46–63.

FRANK LLOYD WRIGHT'S OWN HOUSES

10. For Wright's own assessment of Sullivan's influence on his work, see Frank Lloyd Wright, "In the Cause of Architecture," *Architectural Record* 23 (March 1908) : 156; and Wright, *Genius and the Mobocracy,* passim. See also Robert C. Spencer, Jr., "The Work of Frank Lloyd Wright," *Architectural Review* (Boston) 7 (June 1900) : 65–67.

11. Frank Lloyd Wright, "Recollections: United States, 1893–1920," *Architects' Journal* 84 (30 July 1936) : 142.

12. For a summary of Wright's beliefs in this regard, see Frank Lloyd Wright, *An Autobiography* (London: Longmans, Green, and Company, 1932), 136–46.

13. See Donald P. Hallmark, "Richard W. Bock, Sculptor. Part III: The Mature Collaborations," *Prairie School Review* 8, no. 2 (1971) : 5–29. The title of the sculpture is taken from a short poem by Tennyson, which is inscribed on the rear of the piece. The importance Wright attached to the sculpture is attested to by the fact that he published it, first, as the closing image of his major article and retrospective in *Architectural Record* of March 1908 ("In the Cause of Architecture"); then again, in the introduction by C. R. Ashbee to the smaller Wasmuth monograph, *Frank Lloyd Wright: Ausgeführte Bauten* (Berlin, 1911); and, finally, used a second cast of it for the hillside garden of Taliesin (see pp. 34–36 below).

14. Wright, *Autobiography,* 165.

15. Ibid.

16. Frank Lloyd Wright, *Ausgeführte Bauten und Entwürfe von Frank Lloyd Wright* (Berlin: Ernst Wasmuth, 1910), pl. 30. The same plan was later reproduced (though again not referred to in the text) in Henry-Russell Hitchcock, *In the Nature of Materials: The Buildings of Frank Lloyd Wright, 1887–1941* (New York: Hawthorn Books, 1942), fig. 80. For my own, somewhat brief analysis of the plan, see Neil Levine, "Frank Lloyd Wright's Diagonal Planning," in Helen Searing, ed., *In Search of Modern Architecture: A Tribute to Henry-Russell Hitchcock* (New York: Architectural History Foundation/MIT Press, 1982, 249–50.

17. The date of 1903, given in Hitchcock's *In the Nature of Materials,* is bracketed and indicated as uncertain. It is the date given in the Frank Lloyd Wright Foundation publications. If, however, the studio-house was designed after Wright and Mamah Cheney had begun their affair, it might well be of the following year. It might be noted that there is a double rather than a single bed indicated on the plan.

18. One, of course, hardly needs to be reminded that 1910 was the year in which Gropius, Mies, and Le Corbusier were all, at one time or another, in Berlin working in Peter Behrens's office.

19. Wright, *Autobiography,* 168. The house Wright rented is called the

Villino Belvedere and is located on the Via Montececeri, which is a continuation of the Via Giuseppe Verdi. See Anon., "Wright's Fiesole Studio," *Frank Lloyd Wright Newsletter* 5, no. 1 (first quarter 1982): 18.

20. No plan of this house has ever been published, nor does one seem to exist in the Taliesin archives. Two different perspectives of it have been published, the first in Arthur Drexler, *The Drawings of Frank Lloyd Wright* (New York: Bramhall House, 1962), fig. 38; and the second in Alberto Izzo, Camillo Gubitosi, and Marcello Angrisani, *Frank Lloyd Wright disegni, 1887–1959* (Florence: Centro Di, 1976), fig. 27. The aerial perspective reproduced here (fig. 14) was kindly provided to me by Bruce Brooks Pfeiffer.

21. See Bruce Brooks Pfeiffer, *Treasures of Taliesin: Seventy-Six Unbuilt Designs of Frank Lloyd Wright* (Fresno: The Press at California State University/ Carbondale, Ill.: Southern Illinois University Press, 1985), 6.

22. The first two publications of Taliesin were in 1913: Anon., "The Studio-Home of Frank Lloyd Wright," *Architectural Record* 33 (January 1913): 45–54; and C. R. Ashbee, "Taliesin, the Home of Frank Lloyd Wright, and a Study of the Owner," *Western Architect* 19 (February 1913): 16–19. Wright's own description in his *Autobiography* was based on his earlier article, "Taliesin: The Chronicle of a House with a Heart," *Liberty* 6 (23 March 1929): 21–22, 24, 26–29. The most recent discussion is in Walter L. Creese, *The Crowning of the American Landscape: Eight Great Spaces and Their Buildings* (Princeton: Princeton University Press, 1985), 241–78. The most provocative analysis remains that of Thomas Beeby, "The Song of Taliesin," *Modulus, The University of Virginia School of Architecture Review* (1980–81): 2–11.

23. The contrast with the earlier Hillside Home School, built less than a mile away and only ten years before (1901–2), is even more striking. There, the same local limestone was used, but, instead of being quarry-faced, it was rock-faced ashlar laid evenly to produce a smooth, continuous surface. Each block was squared to make tight, definitive joints, and the margins of the corner stones were chisel-drafted to produce a classical appearance of solidity.

24. Wright, *Autobiography*, 173.

25. Ibid., 171, 175.

26. For a more extensive discussion of this phase, see my earlier article, "Hollyhock House and the Romance of Southern California," *Art in America* 71 (September 1983): esp. 160–63. For the most complete account of Wright's wanderings during these years, see Kathryn Smith, "Frank Lloyd Wright and the Imperial Hotel: A Postscript," *Art Bulletin* 67 (June 1985): 296–310.

27. This is the new title Wright gave to the chapter dealing with the

construction of the hotel in the second edition of his *Autobiography* (Frank Lloyd Wright, *An Autobiography* [New York: Duell, Sloan and Pearce, 1943], 213). This second edition will hereafter be referred to as *Autobiography* (1943).

28. I would particularly like to thank Bruce Brooks Pfeiffer for making this project known to me, as well as for sharing his thoughts about it with me, before it appeared in the tenth volume of Wright's complete works: *Frank Lloyd Wright: Preliminary Studies, 1917–1932,* edited by Yukio Futagawa, text by Bruce Brooks Pfeiffer (Tokyo: A.D.A. EDITA, 1986), 64–65.

29. The date on the drawing is 1921. However, our knowledge of the Death Valley commission is very sketchy. Wright refers in his *Autobiography* (p. 253) to a visit to the site with Death Valley Scotty, but does not indicate a date. We know that Richard Neutra was working on the final drawings of the Johnson ranch project in November 1924. Dione Neutra, comp. and trans., *Richard Neutra: Promise and Fulfillment, 1919–1932. Selections from the Letters and Diaries of Richard and Dione Neutra* (Carbondale, Ill.: Southern Illinois University Press, 1986), 130. The perspective sketch of the ranch project, usually referred to as the "A.M. Johnson Desert Compound and Shrine," is generally dated 1922 (Drexler, *Drawings,* fig. 90). My own research, tentative as it is, leads me to believe that Wright could have visited the site as early as the winter of 1922–23, although the following one is more likely. Johnson supplied Wright with indications of the contours of the site in March 1924. For her help in sorting out some of these problems, I should like to thank Susan Buchel, Museum Curator, Scotty's Castle. It should, of course, be remembered that A.M. Johnson was the client for whom Wright also designed the National Life Insurance Company skyscraper for Water Tower Square in Chicago (c. 1924).

30. The plan is quite similar to a number of the small shore cottages and houseboats Wright was designing at about the same time for the Lake Tahoe Summer Colony at Emerald Bay, California (1922–23). The general shape of the toplit, octagonal building, typologically related to the traditional baptistry, also recalls certain aspects of the studio-library complex Wright added to his Oak Park house in the 1890's.

31. The "defensiveness" of Wright's houses of the early 1920s has often been remarked on. See Norris Kelly Smith, *Frank Lloyd Wright: A Study in Architectural Content,* 2d. rev. ed (Watkins Glen, N.Y.: American Life Foundation & Study Institute, 1979), 125–27. For my own interpretation, see my "Hollyhock House," 153–63.

32. Frank Lloyd Wright, "Taliesin III," June 8, 1926, TS. XXI/4, John Lloyd Wright Collection, Avery Library, Columbia University, New York.

33. Commenting a few years later on this spatial model of architecture, Wright noted: "This interior conception took architecture entirely away from sculpture, away from painting and entirely away from architecture as it had been known in the antique. The building now became a creation of interior-space in light." Frank Lloyd Wright, *Two Lectures on Architecture* (Chicago: The Art Institute of Chicago, 1931), 25–26. And again in 1939, referring to Lao-tse's metaphor of the water pitcher in Okakura's *Book of Tea* as proving "that the reality of the building consisted not in the four walls and the roof but inhered in the space within," Wright added: "That idea is entire reversal of all pagan—'Classic'—ideals of building whatsoever. If you accept that concept of building classical-architecture falls dead to the ground. An entirely new concept has entered the mind of the architect and the life of his people." Frank Lloyd Wright, *An Organic Architecture: The Architecture of Democracy,* The Sir George Watson Lectures of the Sulgrave Manor Board for 1939 (London: Lund Humphries & Co., 1939), 3.

34. For the classical point of view on the same question, see Antoine-Chrysostome Quatremère de Quincy, *De l'architecture égyptienne considérée dans son origine, ses principes et son goût, et comparée sous les mêmes rapports à l'architecture grècque* (Paris: Barrois l'ainé et Fils, 1803).

35. This is not, however, to deny the important sources in the theoretical literature of the nineteenth century for such "non-architectural," "non-classical" archetypal models. Here, Viollet-le-Duc and Gottfried Semper come to mind, both of whose work Wright was acquainted with. I should like to thank Robin Middleton for stressing to me the connection with Semper's thought.

36. The most useful books so far on the Johnsons and their winter house are: Hank Johnston, *Death Valley Scotty: The Fastest Con in the West* (Corona del Mar, Cal.: Trans-Anglo Books, 1974); Dorothy Shally and William Bolton, *Scotty's Castle* (Yosemite, Cal.: Flying Spur Press, 1973); and, most recently, Richard E. Lingenfelter, *Death Valley & the Amargosa: A Land of Illusion* (Berkeley: University of California Press, 1986). The theory of evolution from basket-making to fired-clay pottery was summarized at just this time by Alfred Vincent Kidder in his *Introduction to the Study of Southwestern Archaeology, with a Preliminary Account of the Excavations at Pecos* (New Haven: Yale University Press, 1924), 49, 118–35.

37. In describing the genesis of this method of concrete-block construction he called "textile-block," Wright likened himself to a "'weaver'" (*Autobiography,* 245) as well as a shell-maker. "Concrete is a plastic material," he wrote, "susceptible to the impress of imagination. I saw a kind of weaving coming out

of it. Why not weave a kind of building? Then I saw the 'shell.' Shells with steel inlaid in them. Or steel for warp and masonry units for 'woof' in the weaving." The final outcome Wright saw as "hollow wall-shells for living in! The 'shell,' as human habitation. Why not?" (*Autobiography,* 235).

It might also be noted in passing that the key landmark of the northern rim of Death Valley, opposite the cut of Grapevine Canyon where Johnson's ranch was to be situated, is the 800-foot-deep pit of the volcanic Ubehebe Crater, whose Indian name was thought to mean "Big Basket in the Rock." Federal Writer's Project of the Works Progress Administration of Northern California, *Death Valley: A Guide,* American Guide Series (Boston: Houghton Mifflin Company, 1939), 48.

38. In Baker Brownell and Frank Lloyd Wright, *Architecture and Modern Life* (New York: Harper & Brothers Publishers, 1937), 23 (chap. 2: "Some Aspects of the Past and Present of Architecture"). It was Bruce Brooks Pfeiffer who pointed out to me that this section of the book, written in collaboration with Brownell, was part of a larger history of architecture Wright began working on after finishing his *Autobiography.* A later reflection of this unpublished manuscript can surely be seen in Iovanna Lloyd Wright, *Architecture: Man in Possession of His Earth* (Garden City, N.Y.: Doubleday & Company, 1962), 50ff.

39. Brownell and Wright, *Architecture,* 24. It should be pointed out that Wright quite consciously wavered between the cave and the tree as primitive man's first abode, finally admitting that "it is perhaps better to say he first lived sometimes in trees and sometimes in stone caves" (p. 23). This is significant for it represented in Wright's thought a difference between those who lived in the north, which "always demanded most from [man] in the way of building," and those in the south, where "the builder was satisfied with some grass and leaves raised on a platform of sticks, or with some kind of tent that he might fold up and take with him on his horse as he rode away" (pp. 23–24). The cave-dweller became the prototypical man of the north, and the tree-dweller that of the south. Thus, when Wright later had to admit that the traditional, classical wood "hut" in fact preceded the "large clay cave or pot of the cliff-dwellers" ("But previously better forms of houses had come from the sticks that had been conferred upon him by his friendly companion, the tree") to produce "lighter, more scientific house-shapes" (p. 24), Wright was able to maintain the priority of the cliff-dweller for the environment of the "north" he himself was concerned with. In any event, he noted that the southerners' huts "were at first conical" (p. 24).

Wright's mythic history of architecture as reflecting conditions of the

American subcontinent and thus going back to its prehistoric Indian cultures for a model of origins is repeated in his son John Lloyd Wright's short dissertation on the subject:

> Most of the complexities in architecture have arisen . . . from hooking up organic architecture with Old World architecture and then trying to draw lines to separate them. Why not approach the subject in the first place from a purely *American* viewpoint?
>
> Five thousand years ago, in ancient America, lived the Basketmakers. They used baskets for pots and pans, they lined them with clay for ashes, they used them for carrying water, for storage bins, and even for babies . . . . These simple people lived in trees or behind the protecting jut of a rock.
>
> A leader saw that by building a simple structure of branches and trees more protection would be afforded for them and their baskets. Most of them joined together, and for centuries they lived beside their fields in these flimsy huts.
>
> When the huts no longer protected them nor their baskets adequately from the cold winds of winter, another leader, or inventive genius, thought up a new kind of covering. He dug a large hole in the sandy floor of a dry cave and lined it with slabs of stone to make the floor and lower walls of a dwelling. The walls of the hole were carried higher by building them up with layers of large lumps of clay, or with upright poles wattled together with withes and coated inside and out with mud. . . .
>
> When war-loving tribesmen swooped down upon these defenseless people, a need arose for dwellings hidden away. Another genius conceived the idea of building houses high up in the steep walls of the canyon cliffs. They dug out rooms from the soft red sandstone or built little houses in natural caves or on natural ledges. Here they lived in safety and became known to us as the Cliff Dwellers.
>
> This is but a glimpse of the evolution of good, sound architecture. (John Lloyd Wright, *My Father Who Is on Earth* [New York: G. P. Putnam's Sons, 1946], 129–31)

40. Kidder, *Southwestern Archaeology*, 78, 81, 119–23.

41. Frank Lloyd Wright, "In the Cause of Architecture, IX: The Terms," *Architectural Record* 64 (December 1928) : 512. It should be noted that both Vincent Scully and William Jordy have previously remarked on the significance of the container or "vase" in the later work of Wright, though without giving it the representational meaning I have tried to give it nor taking it back to its sources

FRANK LLOYD WRIGHT'S OWN HOUSES

in his work and thought of the 1910s and 1920s. See, e.g., Vincent Scully, *Frank Lloyd Wright,* The Masters of World Architecture Series (New York: George Braziller, 1960), 30; and William H. Jordy, *American Buildings and Their Architects,* vol. 4, *The Impact of European Modernism in the Mid-Twentieth Century* (Garden City, N.Y.: Doubleday & Company, 1972), 353–59. Both Scully and Jordy refer Wright's concept of the spatial container to the aphorism of Lao-tse that Wright loved to quote from the *Book of Tea* in the later years of his life. See notes 33 above and 42 below.

42. Wright, *An Organic Architecture,* 3. The short book by Kakuzo Okakura, entitled *The Book of Tea,* was published in the United States in 1906, two years after its author had emigrated to Boston and five years before he became Curator of Chinese and Japanese Art at the Boston Museum of Fine Arts, succeeding his mentor Ernest Fenollosa. Although Okakura was an important member of the circle around Isabella S. Gardner and his work was quite well known among artists and intellectuals of the time, there is no indication that Wright had read *The Book of Tea* until the 1920s. According to Bruce Brooks Pfeiffer, Wright received a copy of the book as a gift in the early 1920s. One of his first references to it was in 1938 in the January issue of *Architectural Forum* devoted to his work (p. 35). In the London lectures of the following year, he said:

> To go back now for a moment to the central thought of organic architecture, it was Lao Tze, five hundred years before Jesus, who, so far as I know, first declared that the reality of the building consisted not in the four walls and the roof but inhered in the space within, the space to be lived in. (P. 3)

In recounting the circumstances of this discovery, Wright explained how the passage from Lao-tse's *Tao-tê-ching* was not a revelation of something new but rather a confirmation of something that he had been thinking about for quite some time:

> My own recognition of this concept has been instinctive; I did not know of Lao Tze when I began to build with it in my mind; I discovered him much later. I came across Lao Tze quite by accident. One day I came in from the garden where I had been working and picked up a little book the Japanese Ambassador to America had sent me and in it I came upon the concept of building I have just mentioned to you. It expressed precisely what had been in my mind and what I had myself been trying to do with a building: "The reality of the building does not consist of walls and roof but in the space within to be lived in." There it was! At first I

was inclined to dissemble a little; I had thought myself somewhat a prophet. . . only to find after all, that I was an "Also Ran." The message had been given to the world thousands of years ago. . . . So what? I could not hide the book nor could I conceal the fact. For some time I had felt as a punctured balloon looks. But then I began to see that, after all, I had not derived that idea from Lao Tze; it was a deeper, profound something that survived in the world, something probably eternal therefore universal, something that persisted and will persist forever. Then I began to feel that I ought to be proud to have perceived it as Lao Tze had perceived it and to have tried to *build* it! (Pp. 3–4)

What is curious about all this is: 1) that Wright apparently took so long to come into contact with this celebrated work of *japonisme*, especially given his connection to the museum curators and collectors of Japanese prints in the 1910s and 1920s; and 2) that he never quoted Lao-tse's words literally, but always preferred to phrase them in his own way. Perhaps this was because, in Okakura's translation of Lao-tse's "favourite metaphor" of the empty vessel, the positive concept of space was rendered as a negative image of "the Vacuum." Kakuzo Okakura, *The Book of Tea*, ed. Everett F. Bleiler (New York: Dover Publications, 1964), 24. According to Okakura,

He [Lao-tse] claimed that only in vacuum lay the truly essential. The reality of a room, for instance, was to be found in the vacant space enclosed by the roof and walls, not in the roof and walls themselves. The usefulness of a water pitcher dwelt in the emptiness where water might be put, not in the form of the pitcher or the material of which it was made. Vacuum is all-potent because all-containing. (P. 24)

43. Beginning with the discussion of it in his *Autobiography* of 1932, Wright always used Unity Temple as the prime example, in his architecture, of the development of the concept of interior space "*as the soul of the design*" (*Autobiography*, 161). This interpretation contrasts markedly with Wright's earlier descriptions of the church in either compositional, structural, or programmatic terms. And, as Bruce Brooks Pfeiffer has shown, it was only in the 1950s that Wright wrote on the famous interior perspective of the building: "Sense of Space—to be lived in—the REALITY of the building. The big room coming through—the outside coming in." See *Frank Lloyd Wright: Drawings from 1893–1959*, Exhibition and Sales for the Preservation of Taliesin, exhibition catalog from the Max Protetch Gallery, New York (Chicago: The Frank Lloyd Wright Foundation, 1983), 28.

FRANK LLOYD WRIGHT'S OWN HOUSES

44. Ocatilla can also be spelled Ocatillo or Ocotillo. The spelling given here is the way Wright referred to it in all the original drawings and early publications. Two early descriptions appear in Anon., "'Ocatilla': Desert Camp for Frank Lloyd Wright, Arizona," *Architectural Record* 68 (August 1930): 188–91; and Wright, *Autobiography*, 301–8. Although Wright always maintained that the camp was built in the winter of 1927–28, it is now quite clear that it was actually built the following year. Wright received the go-ahead from Alexander Chandler in late September 1928 to complete the plans for his resort hotel, and then a telegram in early January 1929 asking him to come down immediately to begin work on the site. Chandler to Wright, 25 September 1928; and Wright to Philip La Follette, 10 January 1929, Darwin D. Martin/Frank Lloyd Wright Papers, M355, Department of Special Collections, Stanford University Libraries, Palo Alto, California.

Wright left Taliesin with his family and apprentices (a total of fifteen people) on 14 January 1929 and completed the camp before the end of the month. The group lived there until the end of May, expecting to return the following season, an expectation that would be scotched by the stock market crash and Depression that put an end to Chandler's grandiose plans. Although Wright later claimed that "the Indians carted it all away during the winter [of 1929–30] after we had turned our backs upon it," (*Autobiography* [1943], 311), this was apparently not the case. An excellent, recent archeological study of the site quotes a former apprentice of Wright's stating that he thought "the camp stood for ten years following its abandonment, before it was dismantled." See Margerie Green, "A National Register Evaluation of Camp Ocatillo and Pima Ranch," for Genstar/Continental Homes, January 1983, 11–13. I should like to thank Bruce Brooks Pfeiffer for bringing this report to my attention.

In relation to the question of the "abandonment" or "dismantling" of Ocatilla, it is interesting to recall (see note 5 above) that J. Moutschen, a Belgian architect touring the United States in 1930, claims to have been invited, after hearing Wright's Chicago lectures, "to visit the camp [he] lived in sixty kilometers outside Chicago" ("Souvenirs," 42). His following description, in French, clearly refers to the Indiana Dunes area:

> Le lendemain, en partant par la ligne de Gary, j'arrive dans la petite vallée assez morne et complètement déserte où est etabli le camp qui sert de résidence à l'architecte américain et qu'il a amené de Chandler. Une palissade en larges planches disposées horizontalement et peinte en jaune, enclôt sept baraques en bois et plaques de tôle affectées, chacune, à un usage bien déterminé. La baraque atelier—le garage—les communs—le

garde-manger—le bureau et dans un coin, le living-room du maître. Sur le sol, des madriers et des planches servant de pavement. L'effet est assez inattendu, les matériaux sont grossiers, mis en oeuvre de la façon la plus simple et cependant on sent des dispositions très raisonnées et éprouvées par l'usage. Le living-room du maître est bien fait pour déconcerter, il tient de l'auberge espagnole et de la hutte de trappeur de l'extrême Nord. Qu'on se figure une grande pièce très irrégulière: bois d'équarrissage et toiture visibles tels quels—une énorme cheminée en blocs de béton—des sièges trapus et frustes—des peaux et des couvertures dans tous les coins" (ibid.).

Aside from the replacement of the canvas by metal, the changes in color and furnishing, and the addition of concrete-block chimneys, this reads very much like Ocatilla. Was Ocatilla, indeed, reincarnated in the north? The area of the Indiana Dunes was, of course, where Wright's son John was living at the time. Bruce Brooks Pfeiffer has suggested to me that the writer may have been confusing the earlier design with the cabins Wright built for the YMCA in the Indiana Dunes area around 1930.

45. Wright, *Autobiography,* 305.

46. Ibid., 307.

47. Taliesin West was begun in January 1938 and was more or less completed by 1943 or 1944. Wright's plans for such a permanent winter headquarters go back at least to the fall of 1934. See Frank Lloyd Wright, *Letters to Apprentices,* selected and with a Commentary by B. Pfeiffer (Fresno: The Press at California State University, 1982), 25–26. Very shortly thereafter he began making his first inquiries about purchasing land. For early descriptions and views of the camp, see, in particular, "Mr. Frank Lloyd Wright, the Taliesin Fellowship, and Taliesin West," *Arizona Highways* 16 (May 1940) : 4–15; Wright, *Autobiography* (1943), 452–55; and Frank Lloyd Wright, "Living in the Desert," *Arizona Highways* 25 (October 1949) : 12–15.

48. Another design of Wright's of the following year (1939) that has a similarly explicit pot-like character is the Ludd Spivey house project for Fort Lauderdale, Florida.

49. The area was in earlier times occupied by the Hohokam Indians, whose descendants are the present-day Pima. They mainly farmed in the low-lying valley formed by the Salt and Gila rivers; however, they did use such upland areas as Maricopa Mesa as fortified hill sites, seasonal camps, or sites for ceremonial or religious rituals related to hunting and fertility cults. To my knowledge, no archeological study of the Taliesin West site has been published.

FRANK LLOYD WRIGHT'S OWN HOUSES

50. Wright, *Autobiography* (1943), 454.

51. Wright's use of these petroglyph boulders for such expressive purposes should be compared with the "primitivizing" interest in American Indian art, especially its pictographic techniques, evidenced in the paintings of the early 1940s of such Abstract Expressionists as Jackson Pollock and Adolf Gottlieb. This also coincided with a series of exhibitions devoted to the subjects of rock art and American Indian art at the Museum of Modern Art in New York between 1937 and 1941.

52. Following the design of Fallingwater (1934–37), with its superimposed "trays" reflecting and imaging the movement of water below, there is the Johnson Wax Company headquarters (1936–39); the Ralph Jester house project, the first Monona Terrace project, and the master plan for Florida Southern College (all 1938); the Ludd Spivey house project (1939); the Lloyd Burlingham house project (1940–42); and finally the "solar hemicycle" house for Herbert Jacobs, designed in 1943–44, just slightly later than the Guggenheim Museum. For the relation to water imagery, see Scully, *Wright*, 30.

53. In *Architectural Forum* 88 (January 1948) : 137.

54. According to Bruce Brooks Pfeiffer, this was done by Wright in the 1950s.

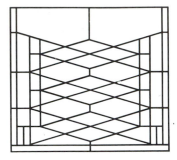

SCHOOLING THE PRAIRIE SCHOOL: WRIGHT'S EARLY STYLE AS A COMMUNICABLE SYSTEM

DAVID VAN ZANTEN

3

It is a truism that Frank Lloyd Wright's Prairie style is abstract, a vocabulary of simple geometric forms without historical or natural reference.[1] His Prairie designs are commonly described as compositions of planes or blocks placed in such loose juxtaposition that they seem to float in relation to each other and to the ground. "In his houses," Sigfried Giedion wrote, "Wright takes the traditional flat surfaces and dissects them in strips horizontally organized and in a juxtaposed play with solid volumes. . . . He dissects the wall and puts it together again with an unprecedented . . . keenness of imagination."[2]

This observation, in turn, introduced the temptation to link Wright's Prairie designs with cubist paintings, executed independently a few years afterward in Europe, and to the open, planar abstraction of the International style, evolving after cubism in the 1920s. Thus Giedion concluded that Wright "is impelled unconsciously by the same forces that worked in Europe about ten years later."

This quality of abstraction in Wright's work is usually attributed to his childhood training with Froebel's modular kindergarten blocks.[3] This childhood experience may be historically dubious. When the anecdote was first set down by his friend Robert C. Spencer, Jr., in his 1900 review of Wright's work, the story is specifically attributed to his teacher-mother, as if Wright himself was doubtful of its validity.[4] Nonetheless, the influence of the kindergarten blocks has proven to be a tremendously resilient myth. The reason would seem to be that while embracing the characterization of the Prairie work as abstract it also evokes another, more rarely expressed Prairie school quality: a sense of assembly, of being composed of modular units which might be arranged in many different patterns, less reminiscent of cubist paintings than of constructions made with children's blocks.

This second quality—modular assembly—is as important as the quality of abstraction. Because Wright has been cited as a precursor and justifier of abstraction in modern art generally, the quality of modular assembly in Wright's work has been interpreted as traces of his effort to achieve geometric purity. Yet this may be putting the cart before the horse, especially when discussing the Chicago school, where the foremost issue was always how one put things together. In what follows, I would like to reverse this paradigm and examine the hypothesis that geometric purity was a means to expedite assembly, achieving a kind of mechanical self-generation in architectural composition.

Wright's Prairie style coincided with his Oak Park studio, the office and drafting room attached to his own house which he organized cooperatively.[5] One of the draftsmen, Barry Byrne, later intimated that Wright had developed a system by which a design could be made to generate itself on the office's boards once Wright had set it in motion with a general layout:

> Endowed as he was with an unerring sense of the third dimension, Mr. Wright, in the period between 1902 and 1909 when I was in the studio, always arrived at his designs in plan and elevation, the last usually the determining one upon which perspectives were based. In the later years of my tutelage, and when projects were turned over to me to develop into working drawings, the original Wright-made studies would come into my hands with the plan established and the main theme of the exterior design clearly defined in elevation. The development of all implied but not delineated portions of the project then became the problem of the student draftsman, subject to the master's approval and often to his correction.[6]

More immediately and more tellingly, Byrne's contemporary in the studio, Charles E. White, wrote a friend in 1904:

Wright's greatest contribution to Architecture, I think, is his unit system of design. All his plans are composed of units grouped in a symmetrical or systematic way. The unit usually employed is the casement window unit of about these proportions. [Sketch] These units are varied in number and size to suit each particular case, and the unit decided upon, is consistently carried through every portion of the plan. His process of getting up a new design is the reverse of that usually employed. Most men outline the strictly utilitarian requirements, choose their style, and then mold the design along those lines, whereas Wright develops his unit first, then fits his design to the requirements as much as possible, or rather, fits the requirements to the design. I do not mean by this that he ignores the requirements, but rather that he approaches his work in a broad-minded, architectural way and never allows any of the petty wants of his client to interfere with the architectural expression of his design. The petty wishes are taken care of by a sort of absorption and suppression within the scope of the plan as a whole, and are never allowed to interfere with the system, or skeleton of the house.[7]

Observing the results rather than the process, the Dutch architect J. J. P. Oud wrote of Wright's work, "Whereas it is a peculiarity of our day, that even the work of the cleverest nearly always betrays how it grew to be as it is, with Wright everything is, without being at all perceptible any mental exertion to produce."[8] Wright himself summarily confirms all this in the same issue of *Wendingen:*

All the buildings I have built—large and small—are fabricated upon a unit system—as the pile of a rug is stitched into the warp. Thus each structure is an ordered fabric;—Rhythm and consistent scale of parts and economy of construction are greatly facilitated by this simple expedient:—a mechanical one, absorbed in a final result to which it has given a more consistent texture, a more tenuous quality as a whole.[9]

In analyzing Wright's Prairie buildings themselves, Richard MacCormac in 1968 observed an irregular grid—a "tartan grid," to use his ex-

SCHOOLING THE PRAIRIE SCHOOL

cellent term—implicit in Wright's Prairie plans, into which the piers defining his spaces are fitted. The tartan grid itself is continuous and indeterminate: Wright can move his pier blocks around within it to define whatever configuration of spaces he wishes. It can be made to organize square, rectangular, T-shaped, or whatever volumes while maintaining unity and harmony. It can be filled in with just a few elements to generate a small house, like the Gale dwelling in Oak Park, or made to organize many elements to produce a large one, like the Darwin Martin mansion in Buffalo. It remains an elastic system with unifying limits and clearly defined axes of development so that compositions suggest their own elaboration. Once a design was "set moving" by Wright, all that his draftsmen had to do was carry it through to completion.

In this context Wright's often reiterated reference to Bach's fugues as his source of inspiration makes great sense. Music is a unit system, and these fugues were specific musical compositions that derived elaborate self-generating configurations from simple arithmetic progressions.

That quality that has been called abstraction in Wright's Prairie work was therefore the manifestation of a self-propelling system of design. As such, it was a posited solution to Sullivan's search for an organic, natural architecture which acknowledged that nature, in building, was necessarily transformed into blocks instead of curves. Wright depicted his own designing of ornament in Sullivan's office as geometricizing, whereas Sullivan's curled and interwove.[10] But we should take this even more broadly: Wright's whole enterprise was the accomplishment of Sullivan's general objectives through geometric means.

To explain this we must examine one of the most pivotal and at the same time most vaguely perceived incidents in the history of the Chicago school.[11] In 1900—when Wright simultaneously set up his Oak Park studio and "discovered" his unit system of design—he and Sullivan, as well as a group of young admirers and sympathizers, were engaged in the formulation and proclamation of an organic system of composition designated by the now forgotten catchword "pure design." Their objective was to create, not individual works of genius, but a whole new school of American architecture, and for a moment they seemed to believe they would succeed.

The story begins in 1885 with the founding of the Chicago Architectural Club, composed of draftsmen not senior enough to be architects in their own right. It became increasingly active in the support of the Arts and Crafts movement during the 1890s, and its executive positions were slowly taken over by its younger members.[12] In 1897, club rooms were made available to them in the newly completed Art Institute building by the director, W. M. R. French. Originally a landscape architect himself, French had already founded an architecture program in 1889 at the Art Institute, headed at first by Sullivan's friend and collaborator Louis J. Millet. Toward the end of 1899, French hired a young architect from Detroit, Emil Lorch, as assistant director to manage architectural affairs at the Art Institute. Lorch, who soon became an officer of the club, joined the other young members of the Architectural Club in mounting an impressive exhibition of their work in 1900, including an Arts and Crafts room and a separate display of the work of Frank Lloyd Wright.[13] The newly emerged Prairie style was prominent in the next two annual exhibitions: the 1901 catalog included Wright's essay "The Art and Craft of the Machine," and the 1902 catalog devoted a separate section to Wright's designs.

At about this same time, in 1899, the club joined a number of other clubs of younger architects in founding the Architectural League of America at a convention in Cleveland.[14] It was a confederation of architectural clubs dedicated to the Arts and Crafts enterprise of creating an indigenous American architecture. "Progress before Precedent" was their motto, and archeological revivalism was the object of their special wrath. Wright was one of the Chicago delegates to the first meeting of the league in 1899 (along with Max Dunning, George R. Dean, Dwight Perkins, Birch Burdette Long, and Peter B. Wight), and Sullivan sent a message that was the "event of the meeting."[15] In 1900 the league held its second meeting in Sullivan's Auditorium Building in Chicago and Sullivan and Wright both gave addresses. During this same period, 1901–2, Sullivan wrote his "Kindergarten Chats" in the Cleveland-based *Interstate Architect*.

In spite of the fact that Sullivan forced Wright out of his office in 1893, they continued to work toward the same end, if not side by side. A group of admirers gathered around them, and all were broadcasting

SCHOOLING THE PRAIRIE SCHOOL

a message meant for a wider audience. What was it? Sullivan's addresses to the Architectural League in 1899 and 1900 and his "Kindergarten Chats" were obtuse, evoking the spirit of a natural, democratic architecture while avoiding specific details.[16] The same was true of Wright's 1900 address, "The Architect."[17] The other addresses to the Architectural League, however, focused on the more concrete problem of principles of architectural design. The Beaux-Arts and the Arts and Crafts points of view were presented.[18] Lorch tried to make a synthesis and coined the phrase "pure design." Basing his ideas on the writings of several contemporary art theorists, he attempted to formulate a purely abstract, geometric system of design. His ideas set the tone for the third convention of the Architectural League held at the University of Pennsylvania in Philadelphia in 1901.[19]

Soon, however, this movement lost its impetus. After 1902 Wright and the Prairie architects were relegated to a more modest position in the Chicago Architectural Club exhibitions and catalogs. Subsequent conventions of the Architectural League were less exciting and fruitful. The league became merely an umbrella organization for architectural clubs, then it faded away. Lorch himself was let go from the Art Institute by French in the summer of 1901. He then went to Harvard to study "pure design" under one of its advocates, Denman Ross, before commencing, in 1906, his very distinguished career as head of the Department of Architecture at the University of Michigan.[20]

In 1908 the young Chicago Prairie school architect Thomas Tallmadge published an article entitled "The 'Chicago School'."[21] It was the first precise use of that now familiar term, applied to the movement which Tallmadge viewed as initiated by Sullivan and carried on by Wright and the Prairie designers.[22] He wrote of the Chicagoans' rejection of historical precedent and of their efforts in the Architectural League:

> Some ten years ago much effort and ingenuity were expended in trying to prove this very thing [that the genius of the American people, the materials at their disposal, and the purposes of their buildings, do not justify the use in their architecture of *any* of the historic styles]. A great deal of time and energy was wasted in

articles and speeches, in which the classic style, the Ecole des Beaux-Arts, Broadway, and pretty nearly everything else not in accord with the new dispensation, were attacked and derided. The slogan of "Progress before Precedent" was adopted—a motto as illogical as it was tactless, as it contained the assumption that progress and precedent could not journey together. Like Abbé Sieyes' epoch-making riddle, "What is the third estate?" so our Revolutionary tribunal had its great question, "What is pure design?" The answers filled the columns of the architectural papers for some little time, until it was pretty well demonstrated that nobody knew what it was, but that pretty near everybody was willing to produce a pet theory on the subject. In looking back at this period of agitation, the storm center of which was Chicago and its Architectural Club, it is not hard to see that all of the pleading was on one side. Very little interest and no concern was manifested by the East, and it is largely on this account that the Chicago men have arrived at their present entirely healthy and proper point of view and position. Divorcing themselves from the idea that they were the evangelists of a new dispensation and that their mission in life was to convert the architectural unregenerated and to fill the land with the glories of a new and an American style, they have devoted themselves to the task of justifying their principles by their works [Tallmadge's emphasis]. (P. 71)

Tallmadge ornamented the first page of his article with two photographs of Sullivan's Transportation Building at the Columbian Exposition. In 1927 he used the same image to start his chapter on Sullivan and Wright in his *Story of American Architecture*. Today we think of Sullivan as a skyscraper architect and start the story of his mature work with the Wainwright Building in St. Louis, designed almost simultaneously with the Transportation Building. The Transportation Building was constructed of plaster and staff; its seems a digression to later European critics like Giedion, who perceive Sullivan's contribution to be the formulation of an architecture expressive of steel-cage construction. But Tallmadge is probably right in putting it first: it was in the buildings of the Columbian Exposition that the nation's architects

SCHOOLING THE PRAIRIE SCHOOL

sought to present a new, post-Richardsonian architectural system. In some quarters at the time it seemed that Sullivan had prevailed. This was the demonstration building, the first proclamation of a new Chicago style, and the subsequent skyscrapers were only proof of the elasticity of the vocabulary.[23] There was another architectural system demonstrated at the Exposition as well, of course: the classical revival system of McKim and Burnham. As the lessons of the event sank in, lines were drawn between the progressives, led by Sullivan and an increasing group of adherents around Wright, and the revivalists. By 1900 the progressives thought they had a solution: the principles of the Arts and Crafts movement given architectural substance in "pure design," especially as it was justified by the new work of Wright. There followed a time of great enthusiasm; then, disappointment. The system didn't "gel"; it could not be widely applied. The movement in the end was what it had been at the beginning: Sullivan's and Wright's, with a crowd of imitations of either or both.

Depicted in this way, following MacCormac, Wright's unit system of design seems brilliant and self-sufficient. But it was, of course, only a method of composition, the structure of his architectural music, but not its content. In 1966 Norris Kelly Smith published a study of the social ideals embodied in Wright's buildings.[24] Starting from the Prairie designs, Smith explored the suggestive symbolic content of Wright's spreading, enclosing roofs and his organization of interiors around embracing fireplaces. He examined Wright's profoundly ceremonial and basically conservative way of life and cites Wright's own numerous declarations about the traditional, symbolic qualities in house design. Neil Levine has been carrying this line of research further.[25]

Such emphasis on the social content of Wright's work makes one sensitive to an anomaly in the Prairie vocabulary. While these symbolic elements are palpable and solidly rendered—the roof casting its deep shadows; the fireplace with its arch or broad lintel and masonry—the unit system he uses to compose the space-enclosing walls seems light and ephemeral. The walls are always defined by a dark wooden grid, sometimes enclosing light plaster, sometimes glass openings, implying that the two are equivalent, mere membranes like the screens composing a Japanese interior. This grid is what is left of conventional mouldings in a Wright design. They have been given a radically different form to accomplish a radically different function. Traditionally, the moulding was where the mass and substance of architectural form was made palpable by excavation and elaboration. The mouldings of American wooden houses were placed and shaped to extend this sense of rendered form to timber construction. But Wright's cross sections are all right-angular, making the mouldings read as mere boards attached to the surface, while he plays with the deep shadows that result to make their planes seem to float in an indefinite relationship to each other. These mouldings, which traditionally were essentially horizontal expressions of the thick masonry laid-up wall, are set on end by Wright and linked together in a horizontal and vertical mesh moving through his spaces, measuring them and articulating the voids. The result is that the walls, the mere "prose" of Wright's architecture, "read out" and recede from attention while the symbolic elements, his architecture's content and "poetry," "read in" and insist upon attention.

Wright's Prairie system, then, was not just a manner of spinning out architectural music, but also a way of producing an appropriate vessel for specific social content. This too brings us back to Sullivan. As in the case of Wright, Sullivan's fervent declarations about democracy have been interpreted in terms of the details of his facades, when in fact, as Joseph Siry has recently suggested, we should likewise accept his buildings as frames for modern social life and so look for the content in the voids within.[26]

It is illuminating in this context to examine the response of the draftsmen in Wright's Oak Park studio to his design system. Wright himself seems to have looked upon this office as a kind of school where instruction in his unit system of design not only enabled the staff to be productive employees but also trained them for creative design in a sort of architectural kindergarten. Not surprisingly, most of the draftsmen copied his unit system in their subsequent work, but, sadly, they rarely used it with originality. Even after leaving Wright, they still elaborated his paradigms and imitated his motifs as if they were still in his office. There were two, however, who were especially close to Wright and who responded differently: the principle draftsman and renderer,

Marion Mahony, and the office manager, Walter Burley Griffin.[27] Mahony seems to have been particularly close personally to Wright; Griffin appears to have been the man Wright discussed things with to get them clear in his own mind. Griffin had gone out on his own in 1906. He and Mahony had collaborated in finishing up Wright's work after his abrupt departure for Europe in 1909, and they had married in 1911. Wright later regarded the two with particular scorn, perhaps because they, unlike all of his other "students," tried to appropriate the symbolic language of his art as well as its neutral system of elaboration. Like the sorcerer's apprentice, Mahony and Griffin were not content with learning the master's lessons but had to discover his secrets as well.

Superficially, the work of Mahony and Griffin seems the most individual and experimental of all the studio draftsmen, but, in fact, behind most of their innovations lies a suggestion of Wright's which they merely blurt out. Their Frank Palma house of 1911 seems a strikingly original design, but actually it combines Wright's interest in native American architecture with his use of raised, open rooms with panoramic views (like the Cheyney, Tomek, and Robie houses) and is embodied in somewhat flat concrete pueblo. Again, their Melson house of 1912, in Mason City, Iowa, is striking in the way it projects from a limestone cliff, but its masonry is clearly a derivative of Wright's recently completed (and very personal) Taliesin, which maintains a much subtler relationship to its natural surroundings. Finally, in the 1912 house they designed for themselves in Winnetka, Illinois, Griffin and Mahony adopted a baroque architectural unit system of their own which, in the end, is essentially decorative: the spaces remain closed and conventional.

This is a sad note, but we do not necessarily have to end on it. Mahony and Griffin produced one design which was their real claim to fame and the test of the Chicago school movement: their winning plan in the 1911–12 competition to design Canberra, the new capital city of Australia. If the essential contribution of Sullivan and Wright was to posit architecture's purpose as the enframement of modern life, here was a whole city laid out in the spirit of the Chicago school. The task posed a double challenge: first, to define the content—the functions— of a modern city; second, to find a unit system of design which would be an urbanistic equivalent of Wright's architectural system.[28] Griffin, apparently, conceived the layout of the plan around a lucid diagram of functions. Mahony executed the exquisite plan and perspectives with their monumental Prairie style ensembles. They met the first challenge by placing a lake surrounded with public gardens at the heart of the city, with museum and athletic facilities spread along one bank facing the government buildings terracing up the other. The government group culminates in an open memorial hall, a belvedere topping a low hill from which a star of avenues lead across the city. They met the second challenge by adopting a unit system, though one very different from Wright's. It consists of a series of hexagonal and octagonal cells in the city plan which generate a network of binding avenues along their diagonals while defining separate, humanly scaled quarters. Griffin's great power evidently was organizational, and here, with no direct precedent of Wright's to cramp his thinking, he has laid out a democratic city with clarity and disarming frankness.

When Wright erected the studio wing of his Oak Park house in 1898, he placed his office in the center, with two separate geometric volumes to either side: the drafting room on the east, an octagonal "library" on the west (fig. 3.1). Libraries were the chief resort of historicizing revivalist architects, Wright's proclaimed enemies in his project to create a new, unprecedented American architecture. Why did he give a library such prominence in his studio complex?

The answer may be that this little space was, in fact, much more than a library. It contained very few bookshelves, the walls being mostly cabinets. There were no windows through which one might look out and rest one's eyes. A single table was in the center, its surface amply illuminated by an encircling clerestory around the top of the space. We know from old photographs and from Alfred Granger's description in *House Beautiful* that the room was filled with the beautiful objects Wright collected and displayed at the exhibitions of his early work: Japanese prints and ceramics, dried flowers, medieval and Renaissance bits of decorative art.[29] That is, this room was not a library but a museum-laboratory, a *Wunderkammer* of odd but intrinsically beautiful things. In the context of this essay, I would hypothesize that the room had two

3.1. Octagonal library of the Frank Lloyd Wright home and studio, Oak Park, exterior. Photo by Donald G. Kalec for the Frank Lloyd Wright Home and Studio Foundation.

functions: First, it was a laboratory where Wright hoped to work out for himself the ideas about "pure design" which Sullivan had suggested to him and which Lorch had picked up from them both. Second, it was Wright's "kindergarten" for the studio draftsmen, the place where they, like the children in his wife's kindergarten at the other end of the house, could touch and examine all these beautiful things and thereby absorb spontaneously the abstract essentials of design.

Tallmadge observed that by 1908 the preaching side of the Chicago movement had faded, replaced by a more fruitful concentration on concrete design. This is precisely what seems to have happened in Wright's case: as his Prairie vocabulary matured after 1900, he must have found the need for research in his *Wunderkammer* unnecessary and tedious. He also must have found his efforts to teach his draftsmen unrewarding as they (Griffin especially, after he left the studio in 1906) simply appropriated his style. In 1909 he abruptly abandoned his family and his studio—his six children in his wife's kindergarten and his dozen draftsmen in his own professional "kindergarten"—and retreated to Europe, then to Wisconsin, to think things through again.

SCHOOLING THE PRAIRIE SCHOOL

NOTES

Extensive revision of this paper was carried out during a Visiting Senior Fellowship at the Center for Advanced Study in the Visual Arts at the National Gallery of Art, Washington, D.C. I wish to thank the staff of that institution for all their help and personal kindness. This paper parallels Otto Antonia Graf's recent and monumental *Die Kunst des Quadrats: Zum Werk von Frank Lloyd Wright* (Vienna: Boehlaus, 1983).

1. See for example, H. P. Berlage's remarks on Wright's work in H. Allen Brooks, ed., *Writings on Wright* (Cambridge, Mass.: MIT Press, 1981), 131–33.

2. Sigfried Giedion, *Space, Time and Architecture* (Cambridge, Mass.: Harvard University Press, 1941), 413.

3. Frank Lloyd Wright himself mentions the anecdote in *An Autobiography* (1932; New York: Horizon Press, 1977), 34–36. It has been developed in some detail in Grant Manson, *Frank Lloyd Wright to 1910: The First Golden Age* (New York: Van Nostrand Reinhold, 1958); and Richard MacCormac, "The Anatomy of Wright's Aesthetic," in Brooks, *Writings on Wright*, 161–74, originally published in the *Architectural Review* 143 (February, 1968): 143–46.

4. Robert C. Spencer, Jr., "The Work of Frank Lloyd Wright," *Architectural Review* (Boston) 7 (June 1900): 61–72; facsimile ed. (Park Forest, Ill.: Prairie School Press, 1964).

5. When Walter Burley Griffin from the studio won the competition to design Canberra, the capital city of Australia (see below), he described himself to the Australian authorities as a one-time partner of Wright's. They, upon writing to Wright for confirmation of this, were informed by him that the studio had been organized cooperatively. He politely denied that Griffin had been a true partner.

6. Barry Byrne, "On Frank Lloyd Wright and His Atelier," *Journal of the American Institute of Architects* 39 (1963): 109–12.

7. Reproduced in Brooks, *Writings on Wright*, 83–92.

8. J. J. P. Oud, "The Influence of Frank Lloyd Wright on the Architecture of Europe," *Wendingen*, 1925, 85–86.

9. Frank Lloyd Wright, "The Third Dimension," *Wendingen*, 1925, 57.

10. Frank Lloyd Wright, *Genius and the Mobocracy* (New York: Duell, Sloan and Pearce, 1949), 55 and passim.

11. What follows is noted, but without great emphasis, in Sherman Paul, *Louis Sullivan: An Architect in American Thought* (Englewood Cliffs, N.J.: Prentice-Hall, 1962); H. Allen Brooks, *The Prairie School: Frank Lloyd Wright and His Midwest Contemporaries* (Toronto: University of Toronto Press, 1972);

and Narcisso Menocal, *Architecture as Nature: The Transcendentalist Idea of Louis Sullivan* (Madison: University of Wisconsin Press, 1981).

12. On the history of the club, see Wilbert R. Hasbrouck, "The Early Years of the Chicago Architectural Club," *Chicago Architectural Club Journal* 1 (1981): 7–14; and John Zukowsky, "The Chicago Architectural Club, 1895–1940," *Chicago Architectural Club Journal* 2 (1982): 170–74.

13. See Arthur Huen's review of the exhibition in *Construction News,* March 18, 1900. It was also in 1900 that Robert C. Spencer, Jr., published the first extensive article on Wright's work (see note 4 above).

14. The league published the *Architectural Annual,* edited by Albert Kelsey, in 1900, 1901, 1906, and 1907.

15. Sullivan's message, the list of delegates, and the schedule of events were published in the *Inland Architect,* June 1899.

16. The addresses were published as "The Modern Phase of Architecture," *Inland Architect* 33 (June 1899): 40; and "The Young Man in Architecture," *Inland Architect* 35 (June 1900): 38–40.

17. Published in *Construction News,* June 16 and 23, 1900, 518–19, 538–40, and elsewhere.

18. *Construction News,* June 16 and 30, 1900, for example, published from among the papers delivered at the 1900 convention the Beaux-Arts ideas of A. B. Trowbridge as well as the Arts and Crafts proposals of Elmer Grey.

19. *Inland Architect,* June, 1901, documented this meeting in detail.

20. See the Lorch papers preserved in the Bentley Historical Library at the University of Michigan. French very sadly gave Lorch notice in a touching letter dated May 11, 1901.

21. *Architectural Review* (Boston) 15, no. 4 (April 1908): 69–74.

22. On the origin of the term, "Chicago school," see Brooks, *The Prairie School.* The designation of architectural systems—like "steel-cage construction"—as "Chicago" had been common since 1890 and was already applied to domestic design around 1900, but Tallmadge seems to have attached the label officially and it was used by everyone henceforth.

23. Sullivan described the building thus in a letter to Daniel Burnham of October 16, 1893:

The thought we sought to express in the Transportation Building was this: *An architectural exhibit.*
The thought subdivided itself as follows:
1. A natural, not historical, exhibit.
2. To be expressed by elementary masses carrying elaborate decoration.

3. All architectural masses and subdivisions to be bounded by straight lines or semi-circles, or both in combination, to illustrate the possibilities of very simple elements when in effective combination. . . .
(Quoted in full in William Jordy, "The Tall Buildings," *Louis Sullivan: The Function of Ornament* [New York: W. W. Norton, 1986], 106–8.

24. Norris Kelly Smith, *Frank Lloyd Wright: A Study in Architectural Content* (Englewood, N.J.: Prentice-Hall, 1966); 2d. rev. ed. (Watkins Glen, N.Y.: American Life Foundation and Study Institute, 1979). I find it hard to agree with most of the details of Smith's argument, but the basis—the assumption that Wright had social objectives—is unassailable and timely.

25. Neil Levine has kindly discussed his book manuscript in progess on this subject with me on many occasions. See Neil Levine, "Hollyhock House and the Romance of Southern California," *Art in America* 71 (September 1983): 150–65; idem, "Frank Lloyd Wright's Diagonal Planning," in Helen Searing, ed., *In Search of Modern Architecture* (New York: Architectural History Foundation/MIT Press, 1982), 245–77; and Levine's chapter in this volume.

26. Joseph Siry, "Carson Pirie Scott: Louis Sullivan and the Modern Department Store," manuscript kindly lent to the author and soon to be published by the University of Chicago Press.

27. Barry Byrne, when he was still alive, thus described their functions in the office.

28. What follows is a summary of an essay about to appear in the Art Institute of Chicago catalog *Internationalism and Chicago Architecture*, with a full bibliography about this complex matter.

29. Alfred Granger, "An Architect's Studio," *House Beautiful* 7 (1899): 36–45.

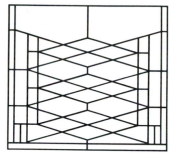

DONALD HOFFMANN

4

When we look at the Robie house, or what it was meant to be and once almost was, we should sense right away that Frank Lloyd Wright was in touch with some great source (figs. 4.1 and 4.2). That source surely was not Vitruvius or Palladio, not the latest arts magazine from Europe or a snapshot brought back from Japan. The house for Fred C. Robie belonged to no historic style or fashion, and as far as Wright was concerned it belonged to no style that should ever be given a name (fig. 4.3). In 1908, the same year that Robie began to plan a house, Wright published the first of his many essays "In the Cause of Architecture." In it he wrote, "I know with what suspicion the man is regarded who refers matters of fine art back to Nature."[1] The same suspicion, of course, abides today. Academic art history almost never bothers with nature. Art is examined as though it can develop only in the tiniest of increments and within a pattern that (with hindsight) is virtually predictable. Art is presumed to nourish itself on previous art, which the historian thus researches, routinely and obsessively, for the presumed "sources." These habits of academic scholarship reduce the creative act to something hardly worth studying. A source as manifold and marvelous as nature finds almost no currency in the intellectual world.

We can see how difficult today it is to understand Wright's buoyant optimism and the depth of his relation to nature when we read the first few pages of his autobiography. For these are small and cynical times. Wright filled these pages with the most lyrical and loving images of nature, making them flicker through his reconstruction of the mind of a

4.1. Frederick C. Robie house, 1908–9, Chicago, ca. 1950.

child. He may have been careless of facts, but it is impossible to believe that he would falsify the central theme of *An Autobiography*. The spirit is much the same as in Whitman's poem:

> There was a child went forth every day,
> And the first object he look'd upon, that object he became,
> And that object became part of him for the day or a certain
>   part of the day,
> Or for many years or stretching cycles of years.
> The early lilacs became part of this child,
> And grass and white and red morning-glories[2]

Wright was nearly sixty when he began writing *An Autobiography*, but it wasn't as though he had turned sentimental. His son John could remember from his own childhood how fond his father had been of weeds; as a young architect, Wright often had ridden his horse from Oak Park onto the prairie to gather weeds that he would carry home and arrange in round copper urns and slender copper vases that were among the very first of his designs for interior furnishings. Sometimes

MEETING NATURE FACE TO FACE

4.2.   Robie house, south aisle of living room, in 1916. Photograph courtesy of Jeannette Wilber.

4.3.   Robie house, living room detail.

4.4.   Evening on the prairie.

he made photographs of weeds; and he even published some of these tender pictures in his special printing of *The House Beautiful,* the tract in which William C. Gannett, the Unitarian minister, praised the faculty for transferring nature indoors.[3] In that same book, to accompany his graphic designs, Wright wrote: "With nature-warp of naked weed by printer-craft imprisoned, we weave this interlinear web." Thirty years later he began his autobiography with an image of the play of naked weed against the snow. Weeds had an amazing vitality and stood as splendid examples of natural patterns in structure. They told of the prairie, where freedom, said Jens Jensen, spoke louder than anywhere else in the world (fig. 4.4). And when, in the *Kindergarten Chats,* the young man in architecture is introduced by Louis Sullivan to nature, he reports: "I like weeds: they have so much 'style' to them; and when I find them where they have grown free they seem most interesting and suggestive to me. I think I'm something of a weed myself."[4]

Yet it is an earlier essay of Sullivan's, from 1894, or the very year to which Wright dated the formulation of his own philosophy of architecture, that provides the key to what Wright set out to be about. Wright's architecture eventually surpassed Sullivan's in at least four

MEETING NATURE FACE TO FACE

4.5. Susan L. Dana house, 1902–4, Springfield, Illinois, detail of butterfly lamp.

basic ways: its level of abstraction; its sense of space and scale; its affection for the nature of materials; and its use of the cantilever—a beam system or slab extended significantly beyond any point of support—rather than the arch, as the most romantic of all structural principles. Wright nevertheless continued to revere Sullivan, because it was Sullivan who had guided him to nature as the source. Sullivan's essay of 1894 expressed two basic ideas about man and nature almost within the same breath. First, he wrote with dismay "that man, Nature's highest product, should alone have gone awry," and then he wrote of the "richness, fullness and variety that might and should come from the man's brain with the impulse of nature's fecundity flowing through it."[5] Man's fall from grace is equivalent to his disharmony with nature. The architect, as a man, is born into the family of nature's highest creatures. If he chooses to "meet modern discoveries, calibers, nature face to face" (to quote Whitman again, in words that Wright chose for his *Architectural Forum* portfolio of January 1938), then the architect can begin to serve as nature's instrument.[6] In short, if nature can be seen as a metaphor of architecture, then architecture can become a metaphor of nature (fig. 4.5).

MEETING NATURE FACE TO FACE

4.6. Robie house, dining room, reprinted from *Frank Lloyd Wright: Ausgeführte Bauten* (Berlin: Wasmuth), 1911.

That is why Wright was willing to take his diploma from nature. He had never done very well at school, and his record at the University of Wisconsin was pitifully meager. Instead, he took encouragement from the men he admired. "Nature is loved by what is best in us," Emerson said. Ruskin wrote that "the disciplined eye and life in the woods are worth more than all botanical knowledge." There was also Thoreau, whose study of nature, according to Emerson, proved to be his perpetual ornament, and whose unqualified dedication to the fields, hills, and waters of his native town had made them known to all reading Americans. Whitman, of course, sang of the open air and of the choice to "no longer take things at second or third hand, nor / look through the eyes of the dead, nor feed on the / spectres in books." Sullivan said it was education's crime to have removed man from nature.[7]

Moreover, nature held the moral corrective to the artificial and debased life of the modern city. Measured against nature, cities were dreary, sterile, confused, unhealthy, ugly places. In 1908 the *Architectural Review* of Boston stated that Wright's gospel was "even more one of social than of architectural regeneration." One reason why the Robie house is so intense and assertive is that it takes the place of lost nature;

MEETING NATURE FACE TO FACE

4.7. Edgar J. Kaufmann weekend house, 1935–37, near Mill Run, Pennsylvania.

it makes up for what Wright called the "barren town lots devoid of tree or natural incident" (fig. 4.6).[8]

Thoreau had worried even about village life. "We need the tonic of wildness," he said.[9] Emerson said cities gave not the human senses room enough, and Ruskin warned that the advantage of living in cities was counterbalanced by the loss of friendship with nature. The function of architecture, Ruskin wrote in 1851, is to tell us about nature. Sullivan said that all great ideas and all great impulses were born in the open air, close to nature. He wrote of "the Great Lake and the Prairie, emblems of pride, fertility and power and graciousness" which "encircle and enfold the city as a wistful mother holds a subnormal child."[10] Wright in his later years remembered Sullivan working on drawings for ornament "in the poetry-crushing environment of a more cruel materialism than any seen since the days of the brutal Romans."[11] Opposite a photograph of his Kaufmann weekend house above the waterfall (fig. 4.7), in his portfolio of 1938, he again chose words from Whitman: "Beware of civilization."

Wright found Chicago to be a piling up of blind forces, an immense stupid gridiron of noisy streets, dirty, dim, and smoky; just the kind of

4.8. Dana house, breakfast room detail.

4.9. Dana house, window detail.

industrial city that had moved Ruskin to say that everything was being made except men, and there was not so much a division of labor but a division of men into small fragments and crumbs of life. Wright looked to nature to sustain his humanity, even his manliness in architecture, and that is why his work should not be confused with the Arts and Crafts movement. The difference is virtually one of gender (fig. 4.8). Charles E. White, Jr., was busy in Wright's studio with the working drawings for Unity Temple, in 1906, when he predicted that the building would be widely criticized, yet would live on. "It has a virile quality," he wrote, "that cannot die."[12] He was right, of course. Wright found in nature only the most definite, the most fully developed strokes, those most free from compromise. The Robie house tells us that much.

From nature Wright also learned about the generous, the luxuriant. Emerson observed the profusion and prodigality of nature, and declared that exaggeration was in the course of things. Ruskin said that the exuberance of Gothic architecture was part of its humility, because no architecture was so haughty as that which disdained "either by the complexity or the attractiveness of its features, to embarrass our investigation, or betray us into delight."[13] Thoreau gave thanks for the wild, luxuriant beauty of nature. "How ample and generous was nature!" he exclaimed. "My inheritance is not narrow."[14] Wright was born in the Middle West, where he saw the prairie turned into the most fertile farmland in all the world. Creativity, he came to believe, implied exuberance; and for the human spirit in love with nature's exuberance, the springs of inspiration could never run dry. That aspect of nature was expressed by the elemental poetry of all its structure (fig. 4.9). "Every true aesthetic is an implication of nature," he said. "It is natural to be 'original,' for we are at the fountain-head of all forms whatsoever."[15]

Nature is nothing less than the principle that gives life its form and character, Wright said; nature is not only the source, but the measure. Thus architecture, to be a vital art, must be like nature. Construction must be seen as nature-pattern, and a building must bear the countenance of a completely organized being. It was the sympathy for nature's ways, Wright said, that gave the indigenous architectures of the world their power to speak of "the love of life which quietly and inevitably finds the right way . . . as little concerned with literature or

4.10. Dana house, sculpture in foyer.

indebted to it as the flower by the wayside that turns its petals upward to the sun is concerned with the farmer who passes in the road" (fig. 4.10).[16] Nature was the best and only true guide to scale, proportions, and the right relations of parts to whole and whole to parts. Wright said that in a fine-art sense his designs had grown as natural plants grow.

From his attention to nature, Wright discovered what he took to be another great truth, that nature had style and was beyond fashion. Here he evidently was indebted to a stirring passage in the sixth of Viollet-le-Duc's discourses:

> Style resides in the true and well-understood expression of a principle, and not in an immutable form; therefore, as nothing exists in nature without a principle, everything in nature must have style . . . it should be explained to you why the cat and the tiger, the flower and the insect, have style, and you should be instructed to proceed like Nature in her productions, and thus you would be enabled to give style to all the conceptions of your brain.[17]

As a corollary, Wright thought, any named style suggested a dead formula or a principle no longer operative in modern life. This explains the cryptic note at the end of Wilhelm Miller's tract of 1915 on *The Prairie Spirit in Landscape Gardening*. Miller says that his illustrations have included houses by Louis Sullivan, Robert C. Spencer, Jr., William Drummond, and Wright, and he scrupulously notes that "Mr. Wright declines to give or recognize any name for this work." In a letter recently published from the Taliesin archives, we do indeed find Wright telling Miller that he is unwilling to "wear any tag which will identify me with any sect or system"; that Sullivan never thought or cared about the prairie as an influence in his art and it would be grotesque to call Sullivan the founder of a "Prairie School of Architecture," just as it was equally deplorable for an American university—Miller then being at the University of Illinois at Urbana—to choose to recognize the work of an individual only when it was presumed to have influenced a group.[18] Plainly, to a mind such as Wright's, the notion of a Prairie style, or a Prairie school, smacked of the second-rate. Wright meant to reach

MEETING NATURE FACE TO FACE

4.11. Dana house, wall-mounted lamp.

beyond the fashionable (or what Ruskin defined as complying with the momentary caprice of the upper classes) and beyond the named styles, to style in the most basic sense, the poetic expression of character (fig. 4.11). "Character is nature in the highest form," Emerson had said.[19] Charles E. White, Jr., wrote from Oak Park in 1903 that Wright had told him to stop reading books and to do nothing but study nature and sketch: "He says to continually and eternally sketch the forms of trees—'a man who can sketch from memory the different trees, with their characteristics faithfully portrayed, will be a good architect'!"[20]

Nature furnished the models of style. Style was the poetic manifestation of character, and the true property of character was individuality. Thus nature served, too, in illustrating individuality. Every individual plant, said Jens Jensen, had its song to sing, its story to tell. Wright said that if the purpose of architecture is to present man himself, then buildings should liberate the lives of individuals, and houses should take on the character of the individual in perpetual and bewildering variety. He said he wished to build for the illustrious sovereignty of the individual. Emerson, Ruskin, Thoreau, and Whitman all stood behind him. "Nature never rhymes her children, nor makes two men alike," said Emerson.[21] Ruskin, in one of those peculiar twists so typical of his mind, wrote that individualism belonged especially to the spirit of northerners, which meant that the most noble Gothic architecture, although Catholic, was essentially protestant. Individuality not only was natural but climatic; so we can understand why Wright, a born protestant like Thoreau, took great pride in identifying Taliesin as a "house of the north." When nature sanctioned individuality it also sanctioned an architecture of romance and mystery. Wright said that romance was the operation of freedom in making form controlled only by a sense of proportion; and the mysterious was that which emanated from a whole so organic as to have lost all evidence of how it was made.

Emerson called nature the most ancient religion and said the mind loved its old home. Nature to Thoreau was the perennial source: "We can never have enough of nature," he said.[22] Wright believed that he could find nothing in nature that was not sacred. That nature paid such infinite attention to individuality was the sign that both spoke of the divinity. Wright said that nature-study provided the only source for a

4.12. Creek near Taliesin, Spring Green.

sound philosophy upon which to base a new aesthetic. Man had the potential for serving as one of nature's instruments in asserting the principle of life. Any true work of art embodied the life-spirit, said Wright, and the true architect possessed a faculty for getting himself born into whatever he did, and born again and again in fresh patterns as the new problems arose. Architecture finally was the opportunity for making man's reflection in his environment a godlike thing. Its aim could be nothing less than the creation of man as a perfect follower of nature. By choosing to meet nature face to face, an architect could make ready to embark on the greatest of all excursions (fig. 4.12).

NOTES

This paper is based on the final chapter of the author's study titled *Frank Lloyd Wright: Architecture and Nature* (New York: Dover Publications, 1986). All photographs were taken by the author unless otherwise noted.

1. Frank Lloyd Wright, "In the Cause of Architecture," *Architectural Record* 23 (March 1908) : 155.

2. Walt Whitman, *Leaves of Grass* (New York, 1892), 288.

MEETING NATURE FACE TO FACE

3. William C. Gannett, Frank Lloyd Wright, and William Winslow, *The House Beautiful* (River Forest, Ill.: Auvergne Press, 1896–97); text reprinted in John Lloyd Wright, *My Father Who Is On Earth* (New York: G.P. Putnam's Sons, 1946).

4. Louis H. Sullivan, *Kindergarten Chats and Other Writings* (New York: Wittenborn, Schultz, 1947), 86.

5. Ibid, 195.

6. "Frank Lloyd Wright," *Architectural Forum* 68 (January 1938) : 13.

7. Ralph Waldo Emerson, "Nature," in *Emerson's Essays,* ed. Irwin Edman (New York, 1926), 387; John Ruskin, *Modern Painters,* vol. 2 (London, 1846), 121; Whitman, *Leaves of Grass,* 25; Sullivan, *Kindergarten Chats,* 196.

8. Wright, "In the Cause of Architecture," 157n.

9. Henry David Thoreau, *Walden and Other Writings,* ed. Joseph Wood Krutch (New York, 1962), 339.

10. Sullivan, *Kindergarten Chats,* 110.

11. Wright, *An Autobiography* (New York: Duell, Sloan and Pearce, 1943), 270–71.

12. "Letters, 1903–1906, by Charles E. White, Jr., from the Studio of Frank Lloyd Wright," ed. Nancy K. Morris Smith, *Journal of Architectural Education* 25 (Fall 1971) : 110.

13. John Ruskin, *The Stones of Venice,* vol. 2 (London, 1853), 206–7.

14. Thoreau, *Walden,* 429.

15. Wright, *An Autobiography,* 147; and idem, "In the Cause of Architecture: Fabrication and Imagination," *Architectural Record* 62 (October 1927): 321.

16. Frank Lloyd Wright, *Ausgeführte Bauten und Entwürfe von Frank Lloyd Wright* (Berlin: Ernst Wasmuth, 1910), 1.

17. E. E. Viollet-le-Duc, *Discourses on Architecture,* trans. Henry Van Brunt (Boston: J.R. Osgood and Co., 1875), 179.

18. Frank Lloyd Wright, *Letters to Architects,* ed. Bruce Brooks Pfeiffer (Fresno, Calif.: Press at California State University, 1984), 50–52.

19. Emerson, "Character," in *Emerson's Essays,* 336.

20. "Letters by Charles E. White, Jr.," 104.

21. Emerson, "Character," 338.

22. Thoreau, *Walden,* 339.

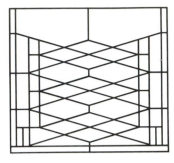

ARCHITECTURAL PRACTICE AND SOCIAL VISION IN WRIGHT'S EARLY DESIGNS

GWENDOLYN WRIGHT

5

A familiar and self-avowed image portrays Frank Lloyd Wright as a resolute individualist, a man who believed that "democracy can live by genius alone. Its very soul is individuality" (Wright 1918, 9).[1] Yet this individualism should not be read as an acknowledgment of the total independence of the self. Wright, like all people, existed in a society. Public and professional matrices significantly affected his development as an architect. The posture of the solidarity genius—which he promoted and architectural historians have largely endorsed—cannot therefore be accepted without qualification. This artist, especially in the early decades of his career, engaged the world around him and it, in turn, engaged him.

As we all know, Wright believed that place mattered. By this, he implied more than simply natural surroundings; he meant as well urban social life and the public exchange of ideas. The 1918 speech, for instance, was delivered at a time when Wright had in fact broken with former colleagues. Yet in this very lecture he insisted that "in a great workshop like Chicago this creative power germinates" (Wright 1918, 4). He went on to praise that city's celebrated poets and playwrights, the educators and journalists of his generation, all men and women he admired. Each of these individuals, Wright declared, sought "to state his inspiration in terms of the character and need of his own time—of his own people; and his work is no less universal on that account" (Wright 1918, 12).

One can do for Wright himself what he called for in his appreciation of John Dewey, Jane Addams, Carl Sandburg, and others; that is, to locate his highly personal and innovative achievements in the larger context of the culture where he lived and worked. Wright's idiomatic statements, his buildings, and his public involvements disclose definite patterns of relation to urban cultural life. The task goes well beyond appraising the individual man, for the premonitions and echoes of his ideas in both the popular culture and the prevailing architectural canon of the time also deserve attention. This approach relies on recent methods of cultural history, in addition to established architectural studies, in an effort to analyze and situate Wright in the public sphere.[2] As Wright asserted in his 1918 speech, this makes the individual artist no less impressive, and sometimes even more so.

In his *Autobiography*, Wright declared that "the real book is between the lines. It is true of any serious book concerned with culture" (Wright 1977, 617). One way to read between the lines is to examine Wright's designs in relation to his specific points of contact with the architectural profession and with the general culture of the cities where he worked. Looking somewhat obliquely at the first major stage of his career, a period that focused primarily on the Chicago area between 1893 and his departure for Japan and California in 1916, one can in fact discern an articulate, highly engaged public persona.

The public dimensions of Wright's work that concern me here cluster in three distinct, but interrelated realms. The first is Wright's relations with the larger cultural milieu of Chicago and the progressive Middle West during his early career. What did he learn from the various groups and organizations concerned with cities, and especially with homes, which thrived there? Why, in turn, did he seek to educate these groups about his own ideas on architectural criticism, pedagogical theories, and political philosophy?

The second realm is Wright's relations with his profession (a topic David Van Zanten insightfully analyzes at length in chapter 3 of this volume). This was a critical time, when Illinois architects debated the stylistic merits of Beaux-Arts civic centers, modern skyscrapers, and the vernacular house design espoused by local builders. In 1897, after seventeen years of lobbying, prominent practitioners convinced the state legislature to enact the first American licensing law for architects,

5.1. Announcement of Frank Lloyd Wright's office, 1898, Oak Park. Avery Architectural and Fine Arts Library, Columbia University.

strengthening their hand over that of builders, engineers, contractors—and clients. Wright recognized the influence of innovators in his discipline—first as a recipient, working with Louis Sullivan; then as a force himself, speaking and writing in several professional settings, sharing both Steinway Hall in Chicago and his Oak Park studio with other young architects of sympathetic bent[3] (fig. 5.1). Here, too, he is more than the ferocious individualist. But despite these positive contacts, Wright felt a profound distrust for the newly emerging profession of architecture, based on the conviction that neither architectural schools nor professional organizations would necessarily embody, or even uphold, the lofty goals he set for the ideal architect. "The architect is something yet to be classified," he told a group of fellow critics in 1900, "though he is tagged with a license in Illinois. So is the banana peddler and the chiropodist" (Wright 1900a, 124; 1900b, 3).

Third, of course, are the designs Wright undertook during this time which belong to the "public realm," both executed work and projects. These include commissions for multiple dwellings; office buildings; clubs, resorts, and pleasure gardens; religious buildings; commercial structures; and, finally, several variations of neighborhood plans which grouped private and public structures together. While Wright's best

WRIGHT'S EARLY DESIGNS

5.2.   Wolf Lake Amusement Park, 1895. Copyright © The Frank Lloyd Wright Foundation 1942.

known work from this period is certainly his many single-family Prairie Houses, these other building types were by no means rare occurrences, nor were they insignificant. In them, Wright tried to formulate his principles about recreation and education, work and leisure, community and privacy (fig. 5.2).

In order to understand Wright's personal connections to public life in Chicago and his architectural prescriptions for the public world, one has to understand how he saw the public and private spheres in relation to each other. This involves analyzing both his life and his work. He did not yet want to separate himself as a private individual or as an artist from the public world; nor did he see the private house as a resolutely isolated, self-contained phenomenon. The design of such dwellings, and especially their possible siting in a residential community, had public connotations. Domestic architecture—for him and for all of us—does not necessarily imply a denial of or alternative to public buildings or public spaces, but rather a full vision of human experience which relates the two realms of public and private life.

Of course, in his own personal life Wright failed to reconcile the tension between individual freedom, family ties, and community mores, eventually fleeing his wife and children in 1909. He seemed sufficiently

WRIGHT'S EARLY DESIGNS

aware of the conflicts in his own life never to suggest that his own behavior represented a real solution for others. Even as he idealized home and family, Wright tried not to pose a radical split between the private and public world, realizing the difficulties this would present.

The commitment to what Wright later called "the *sense of shelter*" (Wright 1977, 166) did not represent an aversion to public life or a lack of interest in settings designed for public activities—even in primarily residential suburbs. Instead, Wright distinctly understood the close interrelation between the public and private, between inside and outside the home—a theme of great importance to the progressives who spoke of "domesticating politics," "urban housekeeping," and "democratic homes" in planned communities.[4]

To be sure, Wright also saw the Prairie House as a haven, even a sanctum, for familial intimacy. Architecturally, he represented this concept in the low sheltering roof, the central hearth, the protected front facade and entrance. These features figure prominently in all of Wright's single-family domestic designs from this period, not least of which is the Robie house. His efforts to give strong visual expression to the idea of family togetherness drew directly from nineteenth-century associationist theories, notably John Ruskin, and from popular American literature on what is now called the "cult of domesticity." However, in his perception of the home as a place for educating children or encouraging feminine values, Wright went beyond the insular focus of most Victorian writings. He did not, for instance, see the beauties and pleasures of home as a means to deter a child's interest in the world outside; quite the contrary, Wright wanted both the formal playroom and the myriad details throughout a house to enliven a child's sense of drama, ambition, and wonder—all of which would be carried into the public world outside the home, much like the Froebel kindergarten theories which seemingly so impressed him as a child. In fact, one can trace a progressive abstraction of conventional domestic imagery in the course of this first stage of Wright's career.

Moreover, a major element of Wright's work involves his consciousness of the changing status of women. In his joint translation of Ellen Key's (1912) feminist tract, *Love and Ethics,* undertaken with Mamah Bourthwick Cheney during their sojourn abroad, Wright extolled the

WRIGHT'S EARLY DESIGNS

modern woman's right to work and productivity outside the home—so long as she did not renege on her duties to those she loved. Much earlier, he had echoed the crusading modernist metaphors of the domestic scientists when he too spoke of the kitchen as "a chemist's laboratory" or "the working department" (Wright 1902, 12; 1901c, 15). Recognizing the work that went on in the home gave this space the worldly aura of a professional setting—although such alterations did not really address women's isolation in their homes. Still, for Wright, the private home did not imply the antithesis of the public world, but rather a complement to it.

There are other ways, too, in which Wright sought to harmonize the public and private spheres, even in commissions for single-family houses. He spoke, for instance, of an aesthetic diversity that would represent and enhance individuality; yet his definition of individuality specifically rejected the Victorian cult of the private dwelling, which had purported that the architecture of each home should reflect something of the owner's taste and personality. Essentially, when Wright endorsed the private home as a form of personal expression, he did not mean it to portray the personal quirks of the client, but rather to show the architect's artistic ability to represent an idealized expression of a class of clients "with unspoiled instincts and untainted ideals" (Wright 1908, 158). The clients' existing home was important to study, "not so much for what it is as for what it may become" (Wright 1901d, 9). Wright believed that the architect should "*characterize* men and women in enduring building materials for their betterment and the edification of their kind"; it was crude commercialism to "give the client what he wants and let him go at that" (Wright 1902, 5). Here then was another ambiguous interplay of private individualism and public mission, in which the architect creates what the clients can only imagine, designing a unique dwelling that would inspire its residents and idealize their role in the larger culture.

It is worth noting that many people in the 1890s recognized the paradoxes of Victorian domesticity: the isolation of women and children in the home now generated a demand for experience outside the domestic sphere that seemed, to some, a sign of the family's imminent demise; the hodge-podge of so many styles, so many flamboyant details, made residential streets seem frenzied, competitive battlefields for attention, rather than peaceful communities. In addition to Wright, other Americans were also looking for a new resolution, both social and architectural, that would give "private architecture" a higher public meaning without destroying its rightful importance to the individual and the family. Journalist Herbert Croly, then editor of the *Architectural Record,* also favored a greater homogeneity in housing; he believed such architecture would be "characteristic of American democracy at its best," because it could strengthen a sense of commitment to the common good, to the public realm over the private (Croly 1903, 199). Home economist Helen Campbell called on architects and housewives to discard Victorian norms for a simpler aesthetic, a less restrictive family life, and a greater participation in civic affairs, especially for women (Campbell 1896a, 98–105; 1896b). Both commentators praised Wright's work in particular, for they recognized his desire to assert the public presence of architecture, even—or perhaps especially—that of private architecture.[5]

Wright did not conceive homes only as individual, detached residences. He was more than willing to think of and design housing *types* which could be duplicated en masse, so that private residences (with distinct variations by socioeconomic class) would become a unified, collective whole, and a context for, rather than an alternative to, public places for the community (fig. 5.3).

Moreover, several of his earliest independent designs involved multiple dwellings rather than single-family houses: the Roloson Apartments of 1894; Francisco Terrace, the Francis Apartments, and the Waller Apartments of 1895. Each showed Wright's ability to balance ornamental details with an elegant, symmetrical massing which gave unity and dignity to the whole. Aesthetically and socially, the larger complexes of 1895 focused on various combinations of central public spaces—garden courts, hallways, and entrances—which shielded occupants from the street and dramatized the points where they came together. Wright's associate, Robert C. Spencer, Jr., describing Francisco Terrace in *The Brickbuilder,* specifically praised the "great courtyard which is treated as a small public garden and on which the majority of apartment entrances face" (Spencer 1903, 182) (fig. 5.4).

WRIGHT'S EARLY DESIGNS

5.3. Quadruple Block Plan. Reprinted from *Ladies Home Journal,* 1901.

To be sure, these commissions came at a time when the city and the nation had entered a major economic depression, debilitating for the building industry and especially for a new architectural firm. The "flat fever" of the 1880s now sustained a weakened housing market, and permits for multiple units surpassed those for private residences in the Chicago area (Hoyt 1933, 215). Yet the projects should not seem any less significant because of these conditions. The aesthetic Wright used was very much in keeping with the social and formal concerns, especially the desire for a simplified facade and harmonious urban design in residential neighborhoods—put forward by such local home economists and housing reformers as Professors Marian Talbot, Sophonisba Breckinridge, and Charles Zueblin, all of the University of Chicago's Department of Social Services.[6] In an effort to promote greater efficiency, economy, and community life, they too advocated a more subdued and publicly oriented approach to residential design for both private dwellings and apartment buildings.

Like these Chicago reformers, Wright did believe that residential areas needed to be kept separate from commercial and industrial

5.4. Courtyard, Francisco Terrace, 1895, Chicago. Reprinted from *The Brickbuilder,* 1903.

5.5. Site plan for a model suburb outside Chicago for the Chicago City Club competition, 1913. Reprinted from Yeomans, *Residential Land Development*, 1915.

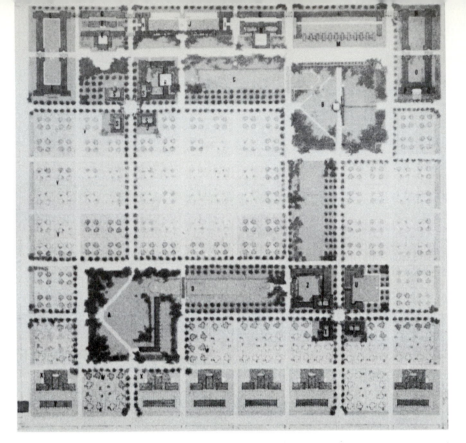

districts. Hence, he designed specific building types for each kind of district or "zone." In the same vein, in 1911, the Chicago City Council, while actively promoting industrial and commercial growth, also limited the right to build or convert for nonresidential purposes in neighborhoods. When, at a more intimate scale, Wright spoke of "protecting" each house and household from its neighbors, the risk to him was the likelihood of an unsightly yard or a pretentious, ugly dwelling next door; he feared an assault on the public side of domestic architecture, rather than the danger of public intrusions on private family life (Wright 1916b, 99). "Individuality is a national ideal," he told European admirers, yet the world of private rights had definite bounds, even in Wright's rarefied vision of American suburbs. The social and aesthetic

WRIGHT'S EARLY DESIGNS

risk of "petty individualism" required skillful residential planning to assure the public of good design (Wright 1910, 65).

If Wright believed in insulating the family and protecting the Prairie House from irresponsible individualism, this did not imply isolation. He understood residential planning in the progressive context of providing all members of a family with access to a variety of public activities.[7] Consider, for example, his noncompetitive entry to the Chicago City Club's 1913 competition for a model suburb southwest of the city (fig. 5.5). Wright's plan featured a range of places for residents to congregate, informally and formally. Settings for outdoor sports were paramount, such as a children's park, playing fields, a gymnasium and natatorium, lagoons for skating, swimming, and sailing. The scheme also contained modern commercial and cultural centers, including a "moving picture building" and a large structure to house the domestic science group with its model kindergarten. The private by no means overshadowed or ostracized the public in Wright's plan. He was familiar with and responsive to these many kinds of public institutions.

Even the street pattern of Wright's community plan stressed a distinctly urban conception. The continuation of Chicago's grid underscored a connection to the larger city, and the groupings of apartment buildings and public places along the periphery created subordinate "business centers" for the 2,582 households living in the proposed new development.[8] While Wright did try to ensure privacy for the well-to-do in a spacious, single-family "Residence Park" (specifying a density there of four houses to the block), he also encouraged social mixing between classes by concentrating the generous public spaces. If domestic architecture was indisputably the central element in the scheme, it was cast in a light similar to the statement of Randolph Bourne, the brilliant young critic on literary and urban affairs for the *New Republic,* when he appraised the Chicago Club exhibit:

> Until architects and engineers, school-children and the average citizen, begin to think of the town or village not merely as a geographical expression or a business enterprise, but as a communal house to be made as well-ordered and beautiful as the

citizen would make his home, social effort will lack a focus, and civic good-will and enterprise be shadowy and unreal. (Bourne 1915, 145)

To be sure, the arrangement of structures and spaces in Wright's proposal involved formal choices, perhaps even more than social prerogatives. While he was unquestionably concerned about the allocation of public and private space and the development of specific building types for different users or kinds of users, Wright concentrated as much on pattern as on community planning in all his large-scale projects. This was true from the first Quadruple Block Plan of 1900 through the Como Orchards summer colony of 1910 and even Broadacre City of the 1930s. Yet the evident tendency to think in terms of formal configurations should not lead us to reduce all social implications to abstract patterns; the two should obviously coexist in good urban design. Wright's conception of urbanity at this time was, in truth, somewhat narrow and artificial, with little real understanding of the problems of poverty, ethnicity, or commercial growth. All the same, public life did imply the diversity and interchange of urban culture, even in an orderly suburb, if the planner wanted a true community. As Wright noted in pencil on an early sketch of the Quadruple Block Plan, "This plan is arranged on the assumption that the community interests are of greater value to the whole" (Wright 1959, 197).

I would certainly not want to suggest by this that Wright trusted any aspect of the public realm without qualification. Both popular culture and public institutions, whether as large as the American Institute of Architects or as local as the Chicago Art Institute, came under his reproach. While the city indeed brought together creative people, he realized that its elite cultural institutions could overly formalize their ability to challenge the establishment, while more populist ones could easily dilute or pass over the most innovative ideas. This situation again suggests Wright's acute sense of the larger cultural issues of the time. Attacks on mass culture resounded with an awareness of what consumer capitalism was doing to vernacular conceptions of beauty and usefulness. "Blame the market if you will," he told the University Guild of Evanston as early as 1896, "but words fail to express proper contempt for the meaningless average household's stuff" (Wright 1896, 5).

Moreover, Wright grasped the fundamental tension between the liberal arena of public life at its best, with open access to new ideas, and the limited sphere of professional life, controlling access to important public responsibilities. Though he revered the "ideal" architect, he recognized the narrowly self-serving aspects of recent professionalization; it was not, in his definition, truly public (Wright 1901d). Not only in architecture, but also in law, medicine, social work, and education, those who sought to consolidate were openly motivated by a desire to restrict outside competition and control judicious experimentation.[9]

When he spoke to fellow practitioners, Wright stressed the need to break the narrow confines of professionalism, to go beyond petty concerns for commercial success and academic correctness. The architect, he implored, should listen to and learn from the public world around him, not only from individual clients and civic organizations, but also from sociological and industrial experts in other fields. Speaking to the Chicago chapter of the Architectural League, soon after he had taken part in founding this group of radical young designers, he insisted that an enterprising professional should work to acquire

> a more intimate knowledge of conditions he is to be called upon to serve. . . . [The] problems of to-day, the problems of transportation, warehousing, city building are his problems. Elevated railway systems and freight stations, manufactures, grain elevators and office buildings, the housing of highly organized industries . . . [the] housing of a people. (Wright 1900b, 11–12)

These public issues, as much social as formal, represented his understanding of professional responsibilities.

Wright hoped that clients and critics would insist on such reform in the profession. He deplored, and thought they should too, the sorry state of the average contemporary architect, whose "duty to the public as professional man [is being] laid aside . . . and merely because the public was ignorant of its claim" (Wright 1900a, 125; 1900b, 3). Acknowledging to a congress of the Central Art Association his own misgivings about "the untrained incompetence of the architectural salesman of today," he called on the large crowd of listeners to place higher demands on architects, and on landlords, too (Wright 1898, 583). The public needed an impetus to take the initiative, and Wright would provide it; together they would force architects to live up to human and artistic standards, rather than mere licensing standards.

In essence, both instances involved a personal dilemma as well as a social critique. Struggling to achieve his high ideals for cultural unity around "the finer forces," Wright denounced selfishness and commercialism wherever he saw it (Wright 1900a, 124; 1900b, 1). As a result, he often lambasted the popular and the professional world around him for not living up to his standards. Whether he spoke of the majority of architects or the majority of homeowners, Wright condemned the tendency of allowing architecture to become what he called "a commodity—a 'thing.'" (Wright 1900a, 124; 1900b, 2; 1901d, 6). His disdain expressed both a personal despair and a larger, quite perceptive analysis of a particular culture at a particular time. Household arts and general literature were indeed highly commercialized, and architects, like other professionals, were being transformed from "a cultured minority integrated with the whole of society to . . . a minority culture" (Heyck 1982, 190). Wright grasped the public significance of both changes.

Conversely, Wright's embittered claim that his own work was disparaged tended to evade reality. To the critics, he later wrote, it "was not only new, but destructive heresy—ridiculous eccentricity" (Wright 1977, 166). Even the title of his second *Ladies' Home Journal* model house of 1901, "A Small House with 'Lots of Room in It,'" suggests a preemptive strike at this perceived popular opinion, a sneer at the middle-class audience which seemed to challenge his aesthetic with commonplace preoccupations. The text, moreover, blamed the "average homeowner" for this design, more conservative than his first house for the magazine, suggesting that he was having to pander to conventional taste. Personality inevitably came into play, as Wright projected counterparts of his own exaggerated emotions—grandeur and scorn—onto an anonymous public. Yet what happened to the architectural profession, to the engaged Chicago public of the progressive years, and to Wright himself such that, by 1914, the popular democracy he had championed in his early speeches had become "the Gospel of Mediocrity," and he could look back on those years as a time when he had been "alone—absolutely alone" (Wright 1914, 412, 406)?

5.6. Fricke House, Oak Park. Reprinted from *National Builder*, 1905.

In reality, both the popular and the professional worlds of Chicago responded early and positively, though never unreservedly, to Wright's house designs. In his profession, Wright enjoyed a surprising amount of respect for a man so young and iconoclastic, as witnessed in the large section of the Chicago Architectural Club's 1902 exhibition devoted to his Oak Park studio, when Wright was only 32 years old, or his one-man show at the Chicago Art Institute in 1907, or the abundant coverage of his buildings and his ideas in the professional press after Robert Spencer's first article in 1900 in the *Architectural Review*. In 1897, just after its founding in Chicago, and again several years later, *The House Beautiful* published laudatory articles on Wright's home and studio and even his aesthetics of flower arranging—somewhat before he came to the attention of architectural magazines.[10] A wide variety of organizations invited him to speak, especially women's groups interested in the arts or in community improvement, such as the Central Arts Association, the College Endowment Association, and the Chicago Woman's Club. Even the local building workers, whom Wright so roundly criticized for their lack of standards, found photographs of his houses, accompanied by positive captions, in the Chicago-based *National Builder* (fig. 5.6), while *Construction News* reprinted his 1900 speech to the Architectural League of America.[11]

WRIGHT'S EARLY DESIGNS

Wright, for all his early devotion to public education and good professional rapport, came to want nothing less than uncompromised authority and total devotion. This became evident in his anger at former associates, first manifested in 1914, when Wright decided that they had reduced his principles to a mere style: "piracy, lunacy, plunder, imitation, adulation, or what you will" (Wright 1914, 410). However, only a few years before he had still spoken positively of Drummond, Griffin, Mahoney, Perkins, Garden, and Spencer as his colleagues in a collective enterprise: "The New School of the Middle West" (Wright 1908, 156). Trusting other designers who espoused the same beliefs—and this could be taken as Wright's criterion for the title of "architect"—he had pleaded with popular audiences to "go, then, to an architect . . . and let this trained artist . . . work out your salvation in mortar, stone and bricks," to trust the "artist, brain of all brains" (Wright 1898, 582; 1904, 107). Early in his career Wright seemed willing to conceive of his architecture in collective terms.

It could be said that when one is defining an artistic position—whether as an architect, a painter or a writer—the surrounding world, both public and professional, seems indeed quite significant. Later, once the philosophy and the persona are formed, the larger world takes on less intellectual importance. In Wright's case, this resolution did not come until the later 1920s, when the magnificent geometry of his California houses and his rural vision of Broadacre utopia first took concrete shape. In a certain sense, Chicago itself seemed to fail him after 1910, as the locus of American intellectual life shifted more toward New York and southern California. Wright too departed for these other regions, despite his plea in 1918 that the "independence of Chicago, her integrity, her destiny as the Capital of the American Spirit, is at stake!" (Wright 1918, 12). But Wright himself no longer believed that the public, even that of Chicago, could be trusted or motivated, except in the most abstract terms of "democracy" or "Usonia"—his new term for authoritarian collectivity.

In the early stage of his career, Wright had wanted to share ideas with the Chicago public and even to pick up cues from popular sources. His lectures sought to create a knowledgeable, critical clientele who would demand, good, modern, "American" work of any architect they might hire. Of course, they should use their knowledge, he contended, to choose the right architect—and then give him total autonomy. All the same, Wright did see the exchange of ideas with popular audiences as an important step in creating the architecture he wanted. In 1898 he pledged to the Central Arts Association, an organization promoting general education in the arts, that "the true place of the artist" is "with the people of average means with a genuine love for the beautiful without a pretense of critical ability, but an innate desire to learn" (Wright 1898, 580). In addition, he wanted "mutual education" between skilled factory workers, artists, and social scientists as the basis of Chicago's Arts and Crafts Society, founded at Hull House in 1897 with Wright as a charter member (Wright 1901a, 68). A belief in the possibility of creating in the city a new moral world, as well as a new physical setting, meant that he needed cohorts, and he sought them in many different milieus.

It would be naive to assume that Wright's engagement with public organizations was only for the purpose of mutual education. Certainly it served to promote himself and his practice. While the search for clients and admirers motivated much of his public speaking, I am willing to argue that Wright's principal goal was moral and artistic education. The architect, he told the Chicago Woman's Club, must "play the part of preacher" (Wright 1902, 1). At the height of his speaking career, addressing the fledgling Architectural League in Chicago, Wright castigated those who join clubs or engage in public speaking before wealthy potential clients in a vainglorious effort to "work the wires for the 'job'" (Wright 1900a, 125; 1900b, 4).

Instead of trying to woo clients with beguiling speeches and pleasant chat, Wright had a mission. He wanted to educate. Elected to the board of directors of the Central Art Association in 1898, he spoke on "Art in the Home" at their annual congress in Chicago that year. "A process of elimination is the necessity now," he explained; "to get rid of the load of meaningless things that choke the modern home; to get rid of them by teaching the teachable that many things considered necessities now are really not so" (Wright 1898, 581).

Wright then went on to elaborate, for the first time, the basic tenets of the Prairie House—even before he had carried them out fully in a design. "I should like to give you a set of golden rules for house build-ing," he told his audience, and thereupon outlined the principles of organic design, simplicity, horizontality, the open plan, natural mate-rials, and integral furnishings. That same year this organization had commissioned Wright, as part of a committee with George Dean and Robert Spencer, to design a model house, "typical of American archi-tecture," to be displayed at the Trans-Mississippi Exposition ("Chi-cago" 1898, 107). While the design apparently did not materialize, the organization's recognition of Wright's significance—and of his poten-tial appeal—closely parallels Edward Bok's decision, three years later, to commission the first of three model houses from Wright for the *Ladies' Home Journal*.[12] In these various instances, as Wright worked out the basic principles and the fundamental design elements of the Prairie House, he did so in conjunction with other architects and closely engaged with the general public.

Even in this context, Wright's goal was not yet self-promotion as a radical new seer, an Olympian individual, for he openly acknowledged that the points he made had become "well-established principles" for popular audiences (Wright 1898, 584). He knew and did not hide the fact that many aspects of his crusade paralleled the recent surge of general interest in reforming housing and house design: the sugges-tions of the domestic scientists, arts and crafts enthusiasts, public health workers, and progressive reformers who dominated Chicago's schools, clubs, and political groups. One such example is Chicago's City Club, where Wright was a charter member of the City Planning Committee beginning in 1908 (after the reform-minded businessmen voted to admit professionals). Here he attended lectures about Euro-pean planning reforms, zoning, industrialization, overcrowding, and improved housing. Around 1911, when Taliesin I was under construc-tion, Wright retired from active participation. As the organization itself was becoming increasingly oriented toward official intervention by ex-perts, rather than open-ended discussion of urban issues, Wright had less in common with its goals.[13]

Before this turn toward expertise, a general debate about urban problems, especially housing reform, infused many settings in Chicago. In the University of Chicago's Sociology Department and the Armour

WRIGHT'S EARLY DESIGNS

Institute of Technology, in the Commercial Club and the Woman's City Club, in numerous artistic and social groups around the city, a wide variety of men and women were talking about architectural change, and Wright had wanted to join in the debate. They strongly endorsed simpler, less obtrusive houses which would supposedly be more healthy and make a minimum demand on the housewife. On a larger urbanistic level, these groups called for lower densities, better use of modern industrial technology, and neighborhood facilities to encourage local civic improvements. Wright incorporated their environmental and aesthetic predilections; he shared their fascination with modern technology; he also responded to the more abstract desires for family stability, community life, the preservation of nature and individuality in modern cities, reiterating the popular progressive belief that these qualities could be enhanced through good domestic architecture. Wright raised the architectural expression of such concerns to a remarkable, unquestionably innovative aesthetic level. But his principles were not as bizarre or disliked or out of place as he sometimes implied.

While Wright did occasionally let fly savage attacks on both popular and professional taste, he wanted reform rather than a truly radical break. He was not, and did not consider himself, an isolated theorist. His goal was a general reorientation of the culture as much as an individual redefinition of architectural style. "You see," he told a meeting of Chicago businessmen as late as 1916 while promoting his partially prefabricated building system, "you in America have been led to believe that an artist is necessarily a queer fellow—one divorced from the life around him. The contrary is true" (Wright 1916b, 122).

Both the means and the guiding philosophy for this reform involved a new synthesis of high culture and popular culture. As Henry-Russell Hitchcock (1944) and Neil Levine (1982) have shown, Wright drew many aspects of his horizontal formality from Beaux-Arts principles of design, while he abandoned the historical styles then so fashionable among the elite and their architects. Likewise, recognizing common chords in the popular appeals for domestic reform in the 1890s—the desire for economical and efficient layouts, space-saving built-in furnishings, modern technology, natural "organic" materials, and a new openness to the outdoors—he emphasized these aspects of his own work. Nonetheless, he made it clear that some facets of vernacular taste, notably the clumsy cult of "simplicity" in the Craftsman or Mission style and the fussy clutter of those who imitated the wealthy, deserved only contempt (Wright 1898, 583; 1901d, 1). Wright's new idiom, as one would expect from a great cultural innovator, drew selectively from the prevailing themes in both popular and high culture, while denouncing others vehemently.

To a certain extent the desire to educate the public, giving their functional and social concerns a more refined architectural expression, sprang from Wright's conception of modern democracy. Sound ideas would flourish, he believed (or at least hoped), if they were freely exchanged, first in discussion and then in building design. Awareness and daring were essential qualities, yet to be effective they had to be unleashed among the larger population, not only among a privileged few. This belief in turn influenced Wright's aversion to an artistic fraternity. He spurned the idea of an academy which lionized an established, old-fashioned elite; nor would he accept the philosophy of "art for art's sake." He instead chastized innovative artists who saw no hope, or at least no potential, in popular American culture (Wright 1901d, 1).

For a time, Wright kept in step with other cultural progressives of the period. Correspondence schools, extension programs, and public lectures proliferated in the 1890s and early 1900s, especially since they could usually offer prominent speakers from a range of disciplines who wanted to reach a general audience with their ideas. John Dewey, for example, like Wright a frequent visitor to Hull House, attacked the sterility of formal education and its detachment from the issues of real life. At this stage, his philosophy of "experimental idealism" sought to strengthen democracy, by which he meant not mere governmental procedures, but individuals involved in community education and community action. "I believe," Dewey declared, "that the individual who is to be educated is a social individual, and that society is an organic union of individuals" (Dewey 1897, 429).

For Wright the key to innovation and social action was obviously formal and spatial. Yet he insisted on the critical role of discourse that could affirm and disseminate new ideas. In "The Art and Craft of the Machine," a lecture presented at Hull House in 1901 at the invitation of

Jane Addams, he stressed the importance of spreading modern ideas about architecture as broadly as possible through the culture, making the most of the printing technology which had revolutionized all aspects of modern life. Wright described the demise, since the Renaissance, of architecture's ancient and noble primacy, due to the growing reliance on the printed text and lithograph, rather than the built form itself, to rally human sentiment. Now, he argued, it was time for the artist to accept these circumstances and to embrace the machine. By this he meant not only using new technology to erect skyscrapers and mass-produced houses, but also creating a new interest in the more abstract problems and potentials of factory production, printed communication, and urban life.

Wright took up these same themes of discourse and education a year later in 1902 when lecturing to the Chicago Woman's Club. Founded in 1876, this organization had become the second largest women's club in the country. Its members now promoted involvement in civic reform, especially where it regarded women, though they still revered art and literature as refined expressions of feminine culture. Adroitly, Wright sensed how to connect his Prairie House program with the audience's dual commitment to reform and uplift, on the one hand, fine art and good books, on the other. Again stressing the theme of general education about house design and domestic life, he repeated his argument about the meaning of public discourse. Words, he said, as well as the designs they described, could teach everyone to demand a level of quality that had once been the province of the very rich. "*The power of types,*" Wright declared emphatically, "*will have translated the beauty of the Cathedral to the homes of the people;* a broadening of the base on which the growing beauty of the world should now rest" (Wright 1902, 4). Once stated and freely discussed among popular audiences, this new domestic aesthetic could then be built, and built in quantity rather than isolated cases. The aesthetic would take hold in popular culture because the architect had demonstrated how closely it adhered to other progressive ideas being talked about at the same time; it resonated. Such was Wright's goal: "to translate the better thought and feeling of this time to the terms of environment that make the modern home" (Wright 1902, 5).

Wright specifically connected his positive, though cautious, image of the machine with his attitudes of the time about urbanity. Joseph Connors, in chapter 1 in this volume, discusses at length Wright's early statements on the city, stressing his use of the familiar progressive metaphor of the city as a "body": a finely tuned organism, but also a projection of the self onto the city's form and its pulsating activities. It is important to realize that this natural imagery of the body was by no means at odds with an equally prolific imagery of machine technology. If, in Wright's words, "the great city" was man's "first great machine, . . . the greatest of machines," it was also, he contended, "at once his glory and menace" (Wright 1901a, 58, 73; 1901d, 16). Again he needed to use *words*—delivering lectures, writing articles, and listening to others—in order to find the right design solutions for the modern city. The goal was both specific and general: to delineate contemporary office buildings and economical dwellings; and then to address the problems of overcrowded streets, inadequate parks, cacophony, and psychological stress. All of this was being done as part of the larger goal of managing, and thereby benefiting fully from, this "greatest of machines," the modern metropolis.

When Wright asserted the issues that preoccupied him at this time—high densities, sprawl, pollution, congestion, anomie—he wanted to tackle them directly in cities and their outlying suburbs. In 1913 he still advocated the familiar progressive tactics of public debate and the use of advanced technology in a decidedly urban setting (one that, typical of the time, included near suburbs as part of a complex metropolitan region), unlike his later schemes of Broadacre City, an isolated, agrarian retreat. This difference is not unrelated to his altered connection, both personal and professional, to the public. By the 1930s Wright saw public relations as a rather simplistic matter of dealing with adoring disciples and antagonistic critics. Earlier in his career the public had meant something quite different: he had indeed been a part of a shared world of mutual education, and he had profited from that complex exchange of ideas.

NOTES

For their helpful comments on earlier drafts of this paper, I would like to thank Thomas Bender, Joseph Connors, and Anthony Alofson.

1. I have occasionally altered the spelling and punctuation of Wright's esoteric style or corrected typographical errors in his manuscripts.

2. Pertinent and interesting examples of this recent cultural history include: Carl E. Schorske, *Fin-de-Siècle Vienna: Politics and Culture* (New York: Alfred A. Knopf, 1980); Neil Harris, *Humbug: The Art of P. T. Barnum* (Boston: Little, Brown, 1973); T. J. Jackson Lears, *No Place of Grace: Antimodernism and the Transformation of American Culture, 1880–1920* (New York: Pantheon, 1981); Elizabeth Kendall, *Where She Danced* (New York: Alfred A. Knopf, 1979); Peter Burke, *Popular Culture in Early Modern Europe* (New York: New York University Press, 1978); Carlo Ginzburg, *The Cheese and the Worms: The Cosmos of a Sixteenth-Century Miller* (Baltimore: Johns Hopkins University Press, 1980); *Faire de l'histoire: nouveaux objets,* ed. Jacques Le Goff and Pierra Nora (Paris: Gallimard, 1974); Richard Hoggart, *The Uses of Literacy: Changing Patterns of English Mass Culture* (Fair Lawn, N.J.: Essential Books, 1957); and Steven L. Kaplan, ed., *Understanding Popular Culture: Europe from the Middle Ages to the Nineteenth Century* (Berlin and New York: Mouton, 1984). Important work is also being done by American scholars studying the social and political roles of popular and folk culture in early modern Europe, most notably Natalie Zemon Davis and Robert Darnton. For an interesting adaptation of these ideas to another American city, see William R. Taylor, "Toward the Launching of a Commercial Culture: New York City, 1880–1939," paper prepared for the Social Science Research Council, New York City Working Group, 1984.

3. On this aspect of Wright's early career, see H. Allen Brooks, "Steinway Hall, Architects and Dreams," *Journal of the Society of Architectural Historians* 22 (October 1963): 171–75. In Chicago, as in New York, Steinway Hall provided space for free concerts and other public cultural activities, in addition to commercial office space, as did the Fine Arts Building, where Wright also chose to set up an urban office.

4. The relation of these themes to architectural design is treated in depth in Gwendolyn Wright, *Moralism and the Model Home: Domestic Architecture and Cultural Conflict in Chicago, 1873–1913* (Chicago: University of Chicago Press, 1980).

5. In "Architecture of Ideas," *Architectural Record* 15 (April 1904): 363, Herbert Croly praised the "new midwestern architects who are departing from tradition," especially Louis Sullivan and "a very able architect, who issued from

Mr. Sullivan's office, Mr. Frank Wright." There is some discussion of Croly's attitudes in David W. Levy, *Herbert Croly of the New Republic* (Princeton: Princeton University Press, 1985), and of Wright in particular on pp. 90–92.

6. See G. Wright, *Moralism and the Modern Home,* and also Stephen J. Diner, *A City and Its Universities: Public Policy in Chicago, 1892–1919* (Chapel Hill: University of North Carolina Press, 1980), as well as the many writings by Professors Talbot, Breckinridge, and Zueblin.

7. Scholarship on the progressives as cultural and political reformers is abundant. Two works that specifically attempt to bring together some of these individuals, including Wright, in order to examine their attitudes about cultural life are Robert M. Crunden, *Ministers of Reform: The Progressives' Achievement in American Civilization, 1889–1920* (New York: Basic Books, 1982); and John Higham, "The Reorientation of American Culture in the 1890's," in his *Writing American History: Essays on Modern Scholarship* (Bloomington: Indiana University Press, 1970), 73–102.

8. Wright's schemes provided for a population of 1,032 families and 1,550 individuals at a minimum, living in detached houses, duplexes, fourplexes, row houses, and apartment buildings for families or single women or men (Wright 1916, 98).

9. On the history of professionalization during this critical period, see, in particular, Thomas L. Haskell, ed. *The Authority of Experts* (Bloomington: Indiana University Press, 1984); Alexandra Oleson and John Voss, ed., *The Organization of Knowledge in Modern America, 1860–1920* (Baltimore: Johns Hopkins University Press, 1979); Thomas L. Haskell, *The Emergence of Professional Social Science: The American Social Science Association and the Nineteenth Century Crisis of Authority* (Urbana: University of Illinois Press, 1977); Mary O. Furner, *Advocacy and Objectivity: A Crisis in the Professionalization of American Social Science, 1865–1905* (Lexington: University Press of Kentucky, 1975); Magali Sarfatti Larson, *The Rise of Professionalism: A Sociological Analysis* (Berkeley: University of California Press, 1977); and Charles E. Rosenberg, *No Other Gods: On Science and American Social Thought* (Baltimore: Johns Hopkins University Press, 1976).

10. "Successful Houses, III," *The House Beautiful* 1 (15 February 1987): 64–69; Alfred H. Granger, "An Architect's Studio," *The House Beautiful* 7 (December 1899): 36–45; reprinted in Joy Wheeler Dow, *The Book of a Hundred Houses* (Chicago: Herbert S. Stone, 1902). (Stone was the publisher of *The House Beautiful* and an avid promoter of the Arts and Crafts aesthetic in Chicago.)

11. *National Builder* 40 (October 1905): 29; 43 (December 1906): 35; 55

(April 1913): 80–83. Fred T. Hodgson, the editor, described the Fricke house as having "a massive look and is somewhat unique in style, but withal quite pleasing." Wright's "The Architect" appeared in the Chicago and New York based *Construction News* 10 (16,23 June 1900): 518–19, 538–40.

12. Edward Bok, *The Americanization of Edward Bok* (New York: Charles Scribner's Sons, 1924), 240–43; G. Wright, *Moralism and the Model Home*, 136–40.

13. The *City Club Bulletin* listed early lectures by George Herbert Mead, Graham Taylor, Jens Jensen, Lawrence Veiller, Benjamin Marsh, Raymond Unwin, and Jacob Riis, among others. By 1910, however, George E. Hooker, speaking on the "Causes of Congestion in Chicago," balanced an appeal for regionalism with the statement: "City planning stands for that *official* application of intelligent design to city growth which . . . shall produce an efficient and at the same time pleasing physical condition" (my emphasis) (*Bulletin* 3 [29 June 1910]: 331).

REFERENCES

Bourne, Randolph. 1915. "Our Unplanned Cities." *New Republic* 3 (June 26): 202–3. Reprinted in *The History of a Literary Radical and Other Papers by Randolph Bourne*, ed. Van Wyck Brooks, 140–46. New York: S. A. Russell, 1956.

Brooks, H. Allen. 1972. *The Prairie School: Frank Lloyd Wright and His Midwest Contemporaries*. New York: W. W. Norton.

Campbell, Helen. 1896a. *Household Economics: A Course of Lectures in the School of Economics of the University of Wisconsin*. New York: G. P. Putnam's Sons.

———. 1896b. "Household Furnishings." *Architectural Record* 6 (October–December): 97–104.

"Chicago." 1898. *The Brickbuilder* 7 (May): 107.

Croly, Herbert. 1903. "New York as the American Metropolis," *Architectural Record* 13 (March): 193–206.

Dewey, John. 1897. *My Pedagogic Creed*. Chicago: E. L. Kellogg & Co.; reprinted in *John Dewey on Education*, ed. Reginald D. Archambault, 427–39. New York: Modern Library, 1964.

Donnell, Courtney Graham. 1974. "Prairie School Town Planning, 1900–1915: Wright, Griffin, Drummond." Master's thesis, New York University Institute of Fine Arts.

Gutheim, Frederick, ed. 1941. *Frank Lloyd Wright on Architecture*. New York: The Universal Library/Grosset & Dunlap.

Heyck, T. W. 1982. *The Transformation of Intellectual Life in Victorian England*. New York: St. Martin's Press.

Hitchcock, Henry-Russell. 1942. *In the Nature of Materials: The Buildings of Frank Lloyd Wright, 1887–1941*. New York: Hawthorn Books.

———. 1944. "Frank Lloyd Wright and the 'Academic Tradition' of the Early Eighteen-Nineties." *Journal of the Warburg and Courtauld Institutes* 7 (January–June): 46–63.

Horowitz, Helen Lefkowitz. 1976. *Culture and the City: Cultural Philanthropy in Chicago from the 1880s to 1917*. Lexington: University Press of Kentucky.

Hoyt, Homer. 1933. *One Hundred Years of Land Values in Chicago*. Chicago: University of Chicago Press.

Key, Ellen. 1912. *Love and Ethics*. Authorized translation from the original German by Mamah Bouton Borthwick and Frank Lloyd Wright. Chicago: Ralph Fletcher Seymour Company.

Levine, Neil. 1982. "Frank Lloyd Wright's Diagonal Planning." In Helen Searing, ed., *In Search of Modern Architecture: A Tribute to Henry-Russell Hitchcock*. Cambridge, Mass.: MIT Press.

Manson, Grant C. 1958. *Frank Lloyd Wright to 1910: The First Golden Age*. New York: Reinhold.

Nye, Russell B. 1951. *Midwestern Progressive Politics: A Historical Study of Its Origins and Development*. East Lansing: Michigan State College Press.

Pawley, Martin, ed. 1970. *Frank Lloyd Wright: Public Buildings*. New York: Simon and Schuster.

Smith, Norris Kelly. 1966. *Frank Lloyd Wright: A Study in Architectural Content*. Englewood Cliffs, N.J.: Prentice-Hall.

Spencer, Robert C., Jr., 1900. "The Work of Frank Lloyd Wright." *Architectural Review* (Boston) 7 (June): 61–72; reprinted, Park Forest, Ill.: Prairie School Press, 1964.

———. 1903. "Brick Architecture in and about Chicago." *The Brickbuilder* 12 (September): 178–87.

Twombley, Robert C. 1973. *Frank Lloyd Wright: An Interpretive Biography*. New York: Harper & Row.

Wright, Frank Lloyd. 1894. "Architecture and the Machine." Lecture to the University Guild, Evanston, Illinois. Excerpts reprinted in Gutheim (1941, 3–4).

———. 1896. "Architecture, Architect and Client." Lecture to the University

Guild, Evanston, Illinois. Excerpts in Wright Papers, Manuscript Division, Library of Congress, and in Gutheim (1941, 4–6).

———. 1898. "Art in the Home." Paper read before the Home Decorating and Furnishing Department of the Central Art Association's Third Annual Congress, Chicago, May. Reprinted in *Arts for America* 7 (June 1898): 579–88.

———. 1899. "The Practical Nature of the Aesthetic." Paper read before the Chicago Architectural Club. Note of speech in *Twelfth Annual Exhibition of the Chicago Architectural Club, Catalogue.* Chicago, 141.

———. 1900a. "The Architect." Paper read before the Second Annual Convention of the Architectural League of America, Auditorium Hotel, Chicago, June 1900. Reprinted in *The Brickbuilder* 9 (June 1900): 124–28; also in *Construction News* 10 (16,23 June 1900); 518–19, 538–40.

———. 1900b. "A Philosophy of Fine Art." (Variation of 1900a.) Lecture to the Chicago Chapter of the Architectural League of America, Chicago Art Institute. Papers, Manuscript Division, Library of Congress.

———. 1901a. "The Art and Craft of the Machine." Paper read before the Chicago Arts and Crafts Society, Hull House, March 6, and the Western Society of Engineers, March 20. Reprinted in *Frank Lloyd Wright: Writings and Buildings,* ed. Edgar Kaufmann and Ben Raeburn, 55–73. New York: Meridian Books, World Publishing Company, 1960.

———. 1901b. "A Home in a Prairie Town." *Ladies' Home Journal* 18 (February): 17.

———. 1901c. "A Small House with 'Lots of Room in It.'" *Ladies' Home Journal* 18 (July): 15.

———. 1901d. "This 'Ideal' Architect." Lecture to the College Endowment Association, Evanston, Illinois. Wright Papers, Manuscript Division, Library of Congress.

———. 1902. "The Modern Home as a Work of Art." Lecture to the Chicago Woman's Club. Wright Papers, Manuscript Division, Library of Congress.

———. 1904. "The Art and Craft of the Machine." (Revised version of 1901a.) Paper read before the Chicago Chapter of the Daughters of the American Revolution. Reprinted in *The New Industrialism.* Chicago: National League of Industrial Art, 1902, part III, 79–111.

———. 1907. "A Fireproof House for $5000." *Ladies' Home Journal* 24 (April): 24.

———. 1908. "In the Cause of Architecture." *Architectural Record* 23 (March): 155–221.

———. 1910. *Ausgeführte Bauten und Entwürfe von Frank Lloyd Wright.* Berlin:

Ernst Wasmuth, 1910. Translated and reprinted as *Buildings, Plans and Designs*. New York: Horizon Press, 1963; Wright's introduction reprinted in Gutheim (1941, 59–76), from which page references are taken.

———. 1914. "In the Cause of Architecture, Second Paper." *Architectural Record* 35 (May): 405–13.

———. 1916a. "Non-Competitive Plan." In *City Residential Land Development: Studies in Planning. Competitive Plans for Subdividing a Typical Quarter Section in the Outskirts of Chicago,* ed. Alfred B. Yeomans, 95–102. Chicago: University of Chicago Press (publications of the City Club of Chicago).

———. 1916b. "The American System of House Building." *Western Architect* 24 (September): 121–23.

———. 1918. "Chicago Culture." Lecture to the Chicago Woman's Aid. Wright Papers, Manuscript Division, Library of Congress.

———. 1959. *Frank Lloyd Wright: Drawings for a Living Architecture*. New York: Horizon Press.

———. 1977. *An Autobiography*. New York: Horizon Press.

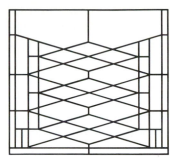

FRANK LLOYD WRIGHT'S OTHER PASSION

JULIA MEECH-PEKARIK

6

Japanese woodblock prints were important to Frank Lloyd Wright for more than sixty years, and their role in his life and work deserves our serious attention. In the first place, Wright was conspicuous as an aggressive dealer in ukiyo-e prints from about the time of his first voyage to Japan in 1905 until around 1923, immediately following the completion of his work on the Imperial Hotel in Tokyo. Among his early letters is the straightforward confession that in the matter of print selling: "I am a merchant and expect to be treated like one—I have little use for the 'gentleman' dealer in works of art. He bores me."[1] It is well known that Wright was a man with expensive tastes who always lived beyond his means. An introspective portrait taken at Taliesin around 1923–1924 shows him clad in elegant velvet breeches and surrounded by expensive and beautiful works of art, including a Chinese marble stele (fig. 6.1). It is not hard to understand why he took as his motto the immortal words of Oscar Wilde: "Let me have the luxuries and the necessities will take care of themselves." It has been said of Wright that he adopted the credit card system long before it came to be sponsored by bankers as the American way of life, and certainly Japanese woodcuts were his primary source of credit for many years when he used them as collateral for loans.

But prints were much more than a business investment for him. They were, in his own words, an "obsession."[2] A passionate collector, Wright hated to part with his fine prints, and his personal holdings still numbered in the thousands at the time of his death. He often wrote about them in philosophical terms, and they affected his attitude toward design. Above all, they were tangible evidence of an exotic, idealized oriental culture that captured his imagination and appealed to his romanticism and love of nature.

THE CONTEXT OF
NINETEENTH-
CENTURY
JAPONISME

Included in the Fine Arts exhibit of the World's Columbian Exposition in Chicago in 1893, about the time the young Wright opened an independent practice in Oak Park, was Thomas Hovendon's sentimental *Breaking Home Ties*, depicting a mother tearfully embracing her young son as he sets off on his own (fig. 6.2). Painted in 1890, it was unquestionably the single most popular painting shown at the fair; the carpet in front of it was literally worn threadbare. Several decades later Wright referred to this painting in a lecture delivered to the Woman's Club of Chicago and published as a booklet entitled *The Japanese Print, An Interpretation*. He contrasted the spirituality of the Japanese woodcut with what he called the banality and vulgar pretense of Hovendon's work, which, in his eyes, could not be called art. An attraction to *ukiyo-e* (pictures of the floating world) was typical of many artists of his generation who were searching for fresh inspiration. Indeed, Wright was far from being a pioneer in the discovery of Japanese prints.

By 1900 Japanese prints already had a long history in Europe, where they had been circulating as early as the 1830s and 1840s. Artists in France and England, especially, were stimulated by their genre themes, bright colors, flattened shapes, unconventional spatial effects, and asymmetrical compositions. Manet and Whistler were among the first to show the effects of Japonisme in their work. Manet's 1868 portrait of Zola, for example, includes not only a folding screen, but also a Japanese print of a sumo wrestler, presumably from Zola's own extensive collection. Whistler's *Golden Screen*, painted in London in 1864 and now in the Freer Gallery of Art in Washington, D.C., attests to his fascination with Japan: he included a folding screen, a kimono, a lacquer box, and a set of single-sheet prints that appear to be from the series *Famous Views of the Sixty-odd Provinces* by Utagawa Hiroshige (1797–1858). By the early 1870s, with his famous series of *Nocturnes*, Whistler had fully ingested Hiroshige's principles of composition and,

FRANK LLOYD WRIGHT'S OTHER PASSION

6.1. Portrait of Frank Lloyd
Wright at Taliesin, ca. 1923–24.
Courtesy of the Kelmscott Gal-
lery, Chicago.

6.2. Thomas Hovendon, *Breaking Home Ties,* 1890. Oil on
canvas. H. 52⅛″, W. 72¼″. Philadelphia Museum of Art: Given
by Ellen Harrison McMichael in
Memory of C. Emory McMichael.
Photograph by Will Brown,
1977.

in turn, had a profound influence on countless artists and collectors at the end of the century, among them Wright himself (see Joseph Connors, chapter 1 in this volume). Monet, who posed his wife in a Kabuki robe against a backdrop of Japanese fans for his 1876 *La Japonaise,* was another early print enthusiast. Some 221 framed ukiyo-e woodcuts are still preserved at Giverny, many of them hanging on the walls exactly as he placed them.[3] Around 1887 Vincent Van Gogh made several slavish copies of Hiroshige prints in oil on canvas. The 400 woodcuts that he and his brother Theo assembled between about 1886 and 1890 are housed today in the Rijksmuseum Vincent Van Gogh in Amsterdam.

During the 1880s and 1890s two ambitious dealers in Paris specialized in ukiyo-e. Siegfried Bing (1838–1905), a German who had become a naturalized French citizen, staged a number of important public exhibitions, and artists including Monet, Degas, Toulouse-Lautrec, Cassatt, Van Gogh, and Bernard found their way to the piles of prints heaped in the attic room of his shop. Bing's chief competitor was the Japanese entrepreneur Hayashi Tadamasa (1853–1906), who imported over 160,000 prints during the 1890s. Hayashi's personal seal appears on many of the fine woodcuts at Giverny.

In the 1890s American Impressionist painters in New York shared a combined interest in both French art and Japanese prints. As early as 1893, J. Alden Weir (1852–1919), Theodore Robinson (1852–96), John H. Twachtman (1853–1902), and others were collecting and discussing the merits of the prints.[4] Weir's *The Red Bridge* of 1895, now in The Metropolitan Museum of Art, is strikingly reminiscent of a composition by Hiroshige that the painter is known to have owned, *Twilight Moon at Ryōgoku Bridge.* Detroit businessman Charles Lang Freer (1854–1919), who bequeathed his renowned collection to the Smithsonian, was converted to oriental art when he purchased five ukiyo-e prints at Boussod-Valladon in New York in 1894, the first year that Americans could obtain good prints locally rather than ordering by mail from Paris. As with his contemporaries (including Wright), prints were Freer's introduction to Japanese art. Freer made his first trip to Japan in 1895 and he soon assembled a substantial group of 400 examples, primarily works by Hokusai and Hiroshige. Because he sold

FRANK LLOYD WRIGHT'S OTHER PASSION

the lot in 1905, Freer's early interest in woodcuts has gone unnoticed. It is worth noting that prints were not inexpensive even in those days: Freer paid $80 for the Utamaro he purchased in 1894. His friend and fellow collector, the debonair New York lawyer Howard Mansfield (1894–1938), later treasurer as well as a trustee of the Metropolitan Museum, observed that Japanese prints are "one of the most notable forms of pure art which the world has ever seen," and cost their fortunate owners as much as they would have had to pay for fine examples of Dürer or Rembrandt.[5]

Artists and collectors alike were beginning to travel to Japan to experience the country firsthand during the 1890s. New York philanthropist Charles Stewart Smith (1832–1909), who made his fortune in the dry goods business, spent his honeymoon in Japan in 1892 and returned with 1700 ukiyo-e prints which he donated to the New York Public Library in 1901. The painter Robert Blum (1857–1903) lived in Tokyo between 1890 and 1892 on assignment for *Scribner's* and acquired some 600 woodcuts, probably intended as reference material for his paintings and etchings of Japanese subjects.

Some artists were drawn to Japan to learn the woodblock technique at the feet of the masters. Arthur Wesley Dow (1857–1922) was probably the most original and successful of early American woodcut artists. Although he did not travel to Japan in search of prints and instruction until 1903, his work during the 1890s was directly inspired by an intense preoccupation with Japanese prints while employed as assistant curator of Japanese art in the Boston Museum of Fine Arts. The exhibition of Dow's own work, color landscape woodcuts, at the museum in 1895 was the first of its kind in America, and he was later the first to teach the technique.[6]

The art school of the Art Institute of Chicago, one of the largest and best in the United States, produced some outstanding graphic artists around the turn of the century. Among them was B. J. O. Nordfeldt (1857–1955), who, although best known as a painter and etcher, also produced a small number of very beautiful color woodcuts in Japanese style between 1903 and 1906. His *Stormy Sea* of 1906 depicts fishermen off the Maine coast, but includes a red title cartouche complete with a

crude attempt at Japanese writing (fig. 6.3). The striated rain falling like a curtain in front of the design and the off-center composition reflect a model by Hiroshige.

Among the significant private collectors of ukiyo-e in Chicago in the 1890s were Charles Morse, Clarence Buckingham (1854–1913), and Frederick W. Gookin (1853–1936), all participants in the historic Japanese woodblock print exhibition at the Grolier Club in New York in 1896.[7] Buckingham was a gregarious and cheerful real estate tycoon who accumulated an outstanding group of about 1400 prints by the time of his death in 1913, and his collection remains the centerpiece of the oriental art department of the Art Institute, of which he was a trustee. He enjoyed hosting print parties at his home, with Gookin presiding as commentator. Gookin had started as a manager at Northwestern Bank in Chicago (a bank owned by Buckingham's father), and his own collection of ukiyo-e, dating from the 1880s, was one of the earliest of its kind in the country. After about 1902 he became a full-time consultant, scholar, and dealer in prints and was responsible for the serious and well-informed cataloging of numerous public and private collections during the 1910s and 1920s, including that of Charles Freer, the New York Public Library, and The Metropolitan Museum of

FRANK LLOYD WRIGHT'S OTHER PASSION

6.4.   Octagonal library, Frank Lloyd Wright studio, Oak Park, Illinois, ca. 1902. Photograph by Henry Fuermann. Platinum print. The Metropolitan Museum of Art, Purchase, Gift of Herman G. Pundt, Ph.D., and Edward Pearce Casey Fund, 1981 (1981.100.17).

Art. His association with Buckingham led to his appointment as curator of that collection at the Art Institute in 1913.[8]

WRIGHT AS DEALER AND CONNOISSEUR

Wright recalled in his *Autobiography* that "during the years at the Oak Park workshop, Japanese prints had intrigued me and taught me much."[9] It is not possible to pinpoint the date of Wright's first contact with ukiyo-e, but their influence is already apparent prior to his first visit to Japan. A photo taken around 1902 of the interior of the octagonal library of Wright's Oak Park studio shows the left-hand panel of an eighteenth-century diptych by Torii Kiyonaga (1752–1815) propped up in the place of honor against the slanted easel of a gate-legged oak print stand (fig. 6.4).

In late February 1905, Wright sailed to Japan for three months with his wife, Catherine, and Mr. and Mrs. Ward Willitts, clients from Highland Park, Illinois, for whom the architect had designed one of the first Prairie Houses in 1902. Wright later claimed that the trip was made primarily in pursuit of prints, but an album of snapshots with which he documented the journey makes clear his paramount concern with Japanese architecture, particularly temple roofs.[10] He did, in any case, return with 213 Hiroshige woodcuts which he displayed the following year at the Art Institute of Chicago, the first ukiyo-e exhibition to be held at that museum and, more remarkably, the world's first Hiroshige retrospective (fig. 6.5).

It is easy to understand Wright's lifelong preference for Hiroshige, whose work is so picturesque, accessible, and even westernized in its use of perspective. In 1925 the British scholar Edward Strange singled out Hiroshige as having had the greatest influence on the West of any Japanese artist. There were actually several American collectors (Judson Metzgar in Chicago and John Happer in Yokohama) who had amassed 3000 Hiroshige each by 1908.

It is clear that Wright used museum exhibitions throughout his life to further his career. The Hiroshige prints in the 1906 exhibition, for which he provided a full catalog, were ultimately sold to Buckingham, for example, and are now among the Buckingham prints at the Art Institute. Only two years later, in 1908, Wright contributed 218 prints to a second ukiyo-e exhibition at the Art Institute (fig. 6.6). Thought to be the largest such display ever mounted in America, there were a total of 655 prints drawn from a handful of local collections, including those of Buckingham and Gookin. They were mounted in six galleries whose design and display were the joint effort of Gookin and Wright. The continuously circulating space and extended vistas are reminiscent of the interiors of Wright's Prairie Homes. The *Bulletin of the Art Institute* for April 1908 described the installation, noting that the walls

> were covered with gray paper having a faint pinkish hue. Against this background the prints, mounted with mats of Japanese vellum or neutral manila board just as they came from the collectors' portfolios, were hung in narrow frames of unfinished chestnut, suspended by green cords that made a charming arrangement of vertical lines across the upper part of the walls. The works of each artist were kept separate but were divided into groups carefully planned for their decorative effect. Additional hanging space was secured, by placing in the larger galleries, screens covered with the same gray paper used upon the walls. These were flanked by posts bearing above, pots of Japanese dwarf trees and azaleas in bloom, and hung below with pillar prints.

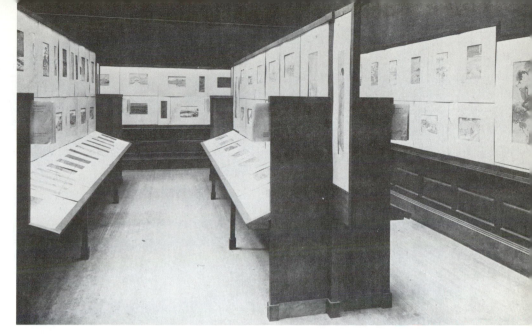

6.5. Exhibition of Japanese prints at the Art Institute of Chicago, 1906. Photograph by Henry Fuermann. Courtesy of The Frank Lloyd Wright Memorial Foundation.

6.6. Exhibition of Japanese prints at the Art Institute of Chicago, March 1908. Courtesy of The Art Institute of Chicago.

6.7. Living room, Taliesin, Spring Green, ca. 1911. Photograph by Henry Fuermann. Courtesy of The Frank Lloyd Wright Memorial Foundation.

Among Wright's contributions to the 1908 exhibit was the invention of a small mahogany stand for narrow vertical prints, complete with a shallow projecting ledge to accommodate Japanese-style flower arrangements, clearly visible to the right of the doorway in figure 6.6. Photos taken at Taliesin between 1911 and 1914 show that he continued to enjoy the use of such print stands in his own home (fig. 6.7).

In 1908, after visiting Minneapolis, Minnesota, to consult with Francis Little about designs for a new house at Northome in Wayzata, Wright opened negotiations with Edwin Hewitt, president of the Society of Fine Arts (later the Minneapolis Institute of Arts), for a loan exhibition of 200 Japanese prints.[11] The plan fell through, however, in part because of Wright's high insurance valuations ($20,000), but also because new interests had taken him to Europe in 1909. In 1917 the architect staged a sale exhibition of prints and screens at the Arts Club of Chicago in the Fine Arts Building. "There are not enough exhibitions," he wrote in the accompanying catalog.[12] On this occasion he composed the prints upon the walls in groups of three, disregarding chronological periodization in favor of "harmonious and instructive contrasts."

Wright had become a full-fledged dealer during these early years. In the summer of 1908 he sold a group of 62 prints for $2000 to Mrs. Sallie Casey Thayer of Kansas City through the sales gallery of the Chicago Academy of Fine Arts.[13] He continued to do business with her as late as January 1911, when they concluded a deal for $10,075 worth of prints. Mrs. Thayer donated her wide-ranging collection, including 1800 Japanese prints, to the University of Kansas in 1917. In a letter of 13 January, 1911 addressed to Darwin D. Martin, for whom he had built a house in Buffalo, New York, in 1904, Wright noted that he had also concluded a successful sale of prints worth $21,000 to Buckingham. These are impressive sums to be sure, but the profits were never enough. Wright's financial problems were aggravated after he left his wife in 1909 to live with Mamah Borthwick Cheney, the wife of one of his Oak Park clients, and then when he built Taliesin in 1911. Correspondence with two of his most loyal clients and patrons, Martin and Little, indicates that by 1910 he was already in debt to Little for $11,000 and had begun the practice of using his prints as collateral for loans. In 1912, for example, he secured a loan of $4000 from Martin with Hiroshige prints valued (by Wright himself) at $8000.

When Wright designed a house, he took charge of every detail, from landscape gardening to interior decoration, and what he liked to see hanging on the walls of his clients' houses were Japanese prints. The clients, of course, were induced to purchase these from Wright himself, and his correspondence indicates that he selected prints for size and color as decorative accents. In 1906, for example, he gave Mrs. Martin specific instructions for dull gold mats for the Hiroshige bird and flower prints in her living room and recommended the purchase of two rose-colored prints by Katsukawa Shunshō (1726–92) for the spaces on each side of the fireplace, where they would complement the green wall:

6.8. Mrs. Darwin D. (Isabelle R.) Martin. Photograph by Müller, 1912. Courtesy University Archives, State University of New York at Buffalo.

My dear Mrs. Martin:

Dimensions for dull gold mats for Hiroshige Bird and Pine panels, for Living Room on brick piers, over capped gas outlet.
Top 7″
Sides 4″
Bottom 8½″
This will make a good sized decoration,—just the thing needed.
For the South Room fireplace I send several from which you may choose. I cannot now find a pair but will look out for another to match whichever you decide upon; or perhaps you will agree with me that it is as well to have them different as they are small anyway and react on a different setting in each case.
Peacock and peony—larger one—
Top 3½″, sides 2½″, bottom 4″.
Smaller peacock—
Top 3½″, sides 2″, bottom 4″.
Plum flowers and birds may be framed to suit the dimensions of the space as it is nearer square. About as it is mounted now is a fair proportion.
You might have them all framed and then select places for them, as they are all pretty sure to work in somewhere.
I send also companion piece to Tokaido.
The Pine and Crane panels are exceptionally fine, in a beautiful state.

Frank Lloyd Wright

N.B. I have wrenched my heart strings and have put in two of my set by the peerless Shunsho, which you may have for the spaces each side the South Room fireplace if you will let me have them some day when I might want to sell the set intact to keep me from going "over the hill." They will be fine, the rose color will be fine with the green wall, and they may be framed thus, if you like:

FRANK LLOYD WRIGHT'S OTHER PASSION

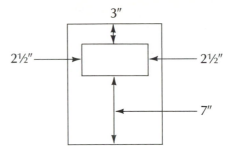

or as they are mounted, reducing the mat to fit the space no more than is absolutely necessary.[14]

In 1912 Wright posed Isabelle Martin in her reception room arranging flowers beside a pillar print (so named for its location in a Japanese home) by Isoda Koryūsai (active 1764–88) (fig. 6.8). The woodcut depicts young lovers rescuing a kite that has been caught in a flowering tree (fig. 6.9). Mrs. Martin's graceful pose and the lines of her pleated gown (probably designed by Wright) deliberately echo those of the figures in the print.[15]

Presentation drawings executed under Wright's supervision around 1906 (the year of the Hiroshige exhibition) also began to show the influence of Japanese design. A rendering of the K. C. De Rhodes house in South Bend, Indiana, by Wright's assistant Marion Mahony (1871–1962) is remarkable for its beautiful and unusual borders of lush trees and foliage, cropped at the sides and hanging over the top like umbrellas, reminiscent of Hiroshige's *Maples at Mamma* from the series *One Hundred Famous Views of Edo*. The insertion of an enlarged detail of bird and flowers in the lower left foreground probably prompted Wright to pencil in the notation: "Drawn by Mahony after FLlW and Hiroshige."[16] Likewise, the perspective rendering of the 1904 Hardy house in Racine, Wisconsin (fig. 6.10), as it appeared in the Wasmuth portfolio, imitates the distinctive shape of a narrow, vertical Japanese pillar print. The house itself is perched dramatically high on a hill, seen from below, with most of the area given over to empty space, very similar to Hiroshige's 1834 composition of a daimyo cortege

6.9. Isoda Koryūsai, *Lovers with Kite,* ca. 1772. Color woodblock print. Darwin D. Martin House. Photograph courtesy University Archives, State University of New York at Buffalo.

climbing toward a castle on Mt. Kameyama (fig. 6.11). The striated sky is a technique often used by Hiroshige to indicate rain, and the branch protruding arbitrarily into the empty center cannot but remind us of Hiroshige's famous *Swallows and Nanten Branch* (fig. 6.12).

Wright's major print client, Buckingham, died in 1913, but that year marked the beginning of the lucrative Spaulding era. Gookin had introduced Wright to the wealthy Spaulding brothers, William (1865–1937) and John (1870–1948), of Boston. The Spauldings, who were just emerging as serious print collectors, invited the architect to their Beacon Street home in January 1913, prior to his second trip to Japan later that month, this time in the company of Mamah Borthwick (the former Mrs. Cheney). It was agreed that Wright would act as their agent, receiving an initial $20,000 toward the purchase of all the unique and superior woodcuts that he could find. The event is recorded by Wright at length in his *Autobiography* with justifiable pride.[17] The following year, after reviewing their new acquisitions, the Spauldings sold several hundred Hiroshige duplicates to the Metropolitan Museum of Art for $17,000, an astonishing price in those days. The sale was negotiated by Howard Mansfield, who had also begun to acquire prints from Wright.[18]

Although he was not officially hired as the architect for the Imperial Hotel until 1916, his old friend Gookin had apparently recommended him for the job as early as 1911 in correspondence with Hayashi Aisaku (1873–1951), the dapper new general manager of the Imperial.[19] Until 1909 Hayashi had worked as assistant manager of the New York branch of Yamanaka and Co., a prestigious Japanese art gallery on Fifth Avenue that sponsored a number of ukiyo-e print exhibitions. It is not improbable that Hayashi had come to know Wright personally during those years. (Wright designed a house for Hayashi in Tokyo in 1917.) Wright sent this letter to Martin on 10 January 1913:

> I am sailing for Japan tomorrow in search of the commission of consulting architect for the new Imperial Hotel, which the government is to own and operate. I have been in touch for some time—almost six months. The Mikado's death postponed affairs and now I have the tip to come on. The building is to cost seven million dollars—the finest hotel in the world.

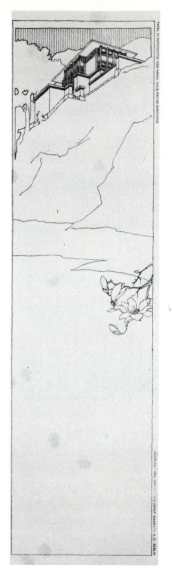

6.10. Frank Lloyd Wright, perspective of Hardy house from Wasmuth portfolio, 1910. The Metropolitan Museum of Art, Purchase, Emily C. Chadbourne Bequest, 1972 [1972.607.49(11)].

Of course I may not get it—then again I may—it would mean forty or fifty thousand dollars and a couple of years employment if I did—so wish me luck.[20]

Between 1916, when he began the Imperial Hotel project, and 1922, when he left Japan never to return, Wright made five extended trips to Tokyo in connection with the design and construction of the hotel. Accompanied by the sculptress, Miriam Noel, whom he was later to marry, he often stayed as long as six months at a time for a total of thirty-nine months, and it seems that every free moment was devoted to prints. The Spaulding money, of which he claimed to have spent $125,000 on the 1913 trip alone, greatly enhanced his buying power in Tokyo; he paid top prices and dealers flocked to his office in the Imperial. "The pursuit of the Japanese print became my constant recreation while in Tokyo," he wrote in his autobiography.[21] He boasted of spending the astonishing sum of nearly half a million dollars on prints during those years, far more than the $30,000 he later estimated as his income from the Imperial project.[22]

Wright's secret weapon in Tokyo was Shugio Hiromichi (1853–1927) who acted as translator and consultant, working on commission for Wright and ferreting out sources of supply (fig. 6.13). Shugio, a distinguished businessman from a samurai family, had been educated at Oxford University and worked in New York as director of an import firm in the 1880s and early 1890s. A connoisseur and collector of ukiyo-e, he befriended Mansfield, Weir, and Charles Freer, among others, and was one of the first members of the prestigious Grolier Club in 1884. Returning to Japan around 1900, he entered the ministry of agriculture and commerce to serve as a member of the imperial commission in charge of overseas Japanese art exhibitions.[23]

Wright was a great theater buff and favored Kabuki actor prints by the Katsukawa artist Shunshō and his pupils Shunkō (1743–1812) and Shun'ei (1768–1819). He boasted that almost all the actor prints in any of the collections of the world were once his—at one time he owned 1,100 Katsukawa-school hoso-e, woodcuts of small size in vertical format.[24] The actor's robes create strong rectilinear and curvilinear designs enriched by bold ornamental patterns that bear a marked resemblance

6.11.　Utagawa Hiroshige, *Kameyama, Clearing Weather after the Snow,* from the series *Fifty-three Stations of the Tōkaidō*, 1833–34. Color woodblock print. The Metropolitan Museum of Art, Rogers Fund, 1918 (JP 517).

to Wright's own aesthetic vocabulary. He was particularly fond of representations of Kabuki matinee idols in the voluminous brick-red garments of the *Shibaraku* (Wait a Moment) role and was attracted by the Ichikawa family crest, an enlarged motif of multiple white squares set off on the actor's sleeves (fig. 6.14).[25] It is the very motif he adopted for the rugs in the Imperial Hotel guest rooms. The rugs have long since disappeared and are now known only in black and white photos, but one can imagine a warm, brick-red color (fig. 6.15).

It cannot be doubted that Wright was a moving force as a dealer in Japanese prints during these years. He had numerous important and discerning clients: in addition to Thayer and Buckingham there were the Spauldings, whose 7000 prints were promised to the Museum of

　FRANK LLOYD WRIGHT'S OTHER PASSION

6.12. Utagawa Hiroshige, *Swallows and Nanten Branch*, ca. 1835. Color woodblock print. The Metropolitan Museum of Art, Rogers Fund, 1936 (JP 2531).

Fine Arts in 1921. Many of the Spaulding prints passed through Wright's hands and are today considered to be among the finest in the world. Howard Mansfield, whose carefully honed collection of 300 prints was acquired by the Metropolitan Museum in 1936, was a regular customer, and the Metropolitan itself purchased some 200 directly from Wright for $20,000 between 1918 and 1922.[26] In 1919 Gookin said of Wright, "I know of no better judge of the quality of prints."[27] The late Yoshida Teruji, an eminent ukiyo-e scholar, reported that when, as a young man, he offered actor prints to Wright at the Imperial, the architect selected only the best. In view of these positive contributions, it is unfortunate that Wright's career as a dealer ended as it did with a nasty scandal stemming from hundreds of "revamped" or reworked prints that were foisted on him in Tokyo around 1920. Wright had already sold the prints to Mansfield and others before being aware of the problem.[28]

As far as can be determined, the architect's subsequent print sales were involuntary ones and occurred mainly during the lean years from the mid-1920s through the early 1930s after Taliesin had twice burned and Miriam Noel was suing for alimony. In 1926 the Bank of Wisconsin foreclosed on Wright's mortgage, taking possession of Taliesin and its contents. To ward off bankruptcy, he was forced to sell 347 Japanese prints at auction through Anderson Galleries in New York City in 1927, a sale that netted $37,000. Old friends like Mrs. Avery Coonley, impelled not only by the beauty of Japanese woodcuts but also by the desire to be of financial assistance to Wright, made purchases at that sale.[29] The following year the bank sold more than 4000 of Wright's prints for a very low price to a local collector, Edward Burr Van Vleck, (1863–1943), professor of mathematics at the University of Wisconsin at Madison. Van Vleck disposed of many of these over the next fifteen years, but the collection as it was bequeathed by his son to the Elvehjem Museum of Art at the University of Wisconsin included nearly 3000 woodcuts, about half of which are said to have belonged to Wright.[30]

In later years woodcuts served a didactic function for his Taliesin Fellowship at Spring Green during the summers. He kept his Japanese prints (as well as his collection of Sullivan drawings) in a locked, fireproof vault adjacent to the studio and his office. (His own drawings, by contrast, were in the studio at Hillside and not in a fireproof vault.)

6.13.   Shugio Hiromichi in Tokyo, ca. 1910–20. Courtesy of Shugio Ippei.

Because of their close proximity to the drafting tables, he would at times bring out prints for informal perusal and talk about them with any apprentices who happened to be passing by. There were also occasional "print parties" in the summer, which are fondly remembered by those who worked with Wright in the 1940s and early 1950s. Curtis Besinger, professor of architecture at the University of Kansas, remembers three or four such parties, one in the summer of 1940, one in 1942 or 1943, and one in the early 1950s. He recalls that these events were planned several days in advance since they required some preparation:

They were preceded by a "sukiyaki" dinner. So some shopping needed to be done to assure that the ingredients were on hand. And the cook and kitchen help needed to cut up the meat and vegetables, etc., to prepare for the meal. And probably the garden crew needed to make sure that they had the desired vegetables gathered and available to the kitchen helpers. Also the small gas stoves which were used for cooking needed to be filled, checked, etc.

The "party" was held in the studio at Taliesin. Everyone sat on the floor on cushions (no tatami!) in groups of four or five people seated around one gas stove. Each group had dishes of meat and vegetables and containers of soy sauce, etc. I think that we had cast iron skillets that we cooked in. Once the "mix" of liquid (don't ask me the make-up of this "mix") began to boil we filled it with meat, vegetables, etc. And waited for it to become cooked. After which everyone helped themselves to a "helping" and more meat, etc., was put in to cook. I assume that there were bowls of boiled rice also available to each group. There may have been "chopsticks." This cooking and eating generally went on until all of the ingredients were used up, including using some of the liquid "mix," which had by then acquired a rich flavor—and was quite tasty over the rice.

After the meal, when the dishes, stoves, etc., were cleared away (tea was always a part of the party, also), Mr. Wright "talked" about the prints. I say "talked." It was certainly not as formal as a

6.14. Katsukawa Shunshō, *Ichikawa Danjūrō IV in the Shibaraku Role,* 1779. Color woodblock print. The Metropolitan Museum of Art, Pulitzer Fund, 1918 (JP 345). Former collection of Frank Lloyd Wright.

"lecture." He must have at at least one or two of these "parties" explained the process of making the prints. And copies of prints in various stages of printing which he showed and explained.

It seems to me that what he talked about were "ideas" or principles that he saw at work in the prints and which he used as the basis for his work. And also, somewhat more nebulous and more difficult to explain, were certain "experiences" that one had from viewing a print which he attempted to translate into three (or four?) dimensional experiences in architecture.[31]

Typically, Wright would line up many impressions of the same subject by Hiroshige for comparison, and standing in front of them, he would discourse for hours, explaining not only the technique of the printing process but also their value for students of architecture. "Well, boys," he said at a print party in 1950, "Hiroshige did, with a sense of space, very much what we have been doing with it in our architecture. Here you get a sense of tremendous, limitless space, instead of something confined within a picture . . . That's a great lesson for you boys to learn." He also told them that Japanese woodcuts would cultivate their sensibilities for landscape:

When you once start with these prints, you never look at nature the same way after. You never have the scene quite the same way as other people who are looking at it who haven't seen these things. A certain natural selection and arrangement takes place in your own sense of the thing as you look. Certain realistic things disappear, and the whole scene becomes more effective and simple because you know this art.[32]

In his 1912 essay, *The Japanese Print, An Interpretation,* Wright praised the Japanese artist's power of geometric analysis. Later in his *Autobiography,* he wrote: "If Japanese prints were to be deducted from my education, I don't know what direction the whole might have taken. The gospel of elimination of the insignificant preached by the print came home to me in architecture."[33] Wright was often observed drawing on woodcuts that he retained in his personal collection. William

6.15.   Guest room of the Imperial Hotel, Tokyo, ca. 1930. Courtesy of The Imperial Hotel.

Wesley Peters, who worked with Wright from 1932 and is now Chairman of the Board of the Frank Lloyd Wright Foundation and Taliesin Associated Architects, remembers that

> Mr. Wright would never have considered altering a fine print in the pristine condition that its creator envisioned. However, I have several times seen him use colored pencils to bring back the miscolored sky or faded "notan" [shading] of a less than good or damaged print that failed to attain the effect that characterized finer examples of the same subject. He also sometimes sketched on poor copies of prints modules or lines that showed the proportion and structure of the concept.[34]

The Wright prints among the Van Vleck collection (presumably never intended for sale) include at least twenty examples on which the architect retraced and extended the lines in the central area of Hiroshige's carefully organized designs. It has been suggested that in doing so he was analyzing the underlying composition of the prints in keeping with contemporary doctrines of "pure design," "a theory of composition that insisted upon the use of simple, geometric elements, such as lines, planes, and regular polygons, and that favored the scrutiny of

FRANK LLOYD WRIGHT'S OTHER PASSION

the geometric structure of Japanese prints."[35] Pure design was developed first in Boston around the turn of the century by Ernest Fenollosa, Arthur Dow, and Denman Ross, all of whom knew Japanese art well and expounded on the possibilities of reforming Western art through knowledge of Japanese composition.

JAPAN AS REFUGE

For Wright, Japan was an arena where he could excel both as an architect (the Imperial Hotel project, for example, came at a time when commissions at home were rare and his personal life filled with misfortune) and as a businessman. He recognized the opportunism of his acquisition of woodcuts in Japan at a time when money was scarce there, but he also had the perception to acknowledge an element of escapism in the lure of the Orient. "I wanted to get away from the United States," he wrote of his 1916 trip to Japan:

> I still imagined one might get away from himself that way—a little. In spite of all my reasoning power and returning balance I was continually expecting some terrible blow to strike. The sense of impending disaster would hang over me, waking or dreaming . . . I looked forward to Japan as refuge and rescue.[36]

Wright's own interpretation of prints betrays a typically romantic nineteenth-century view of Japan as a primitive country, whose people were naive and childlike. It was not contemporary prints depicting the civilization and enlightenment of modern Japan but rather the picturesque landscapes of Hiroshige from the 1830s and 1840s that were preferred by Wright and by most of his fellow collectors in the West. Images of happy peasants in idyllic natural settings reinforced their imaginary vision of "uncivilized" Japan. In his introduction to the 1906 Hiroshige catalog, Wright described the appeal of this artist as

> a spiritual one unlikely to be heard by western materialism with more than amused tolerance . . .
>   The phase of art presented in this collection is that of the artisan class, the common people in the strict sense of the term, and attests the infinite delight, the inherent poetic grace not of the Japanese nobleman but of the hard-worked, humble son of

Nippon of seventy-five years ago. His face was deeply furrowed with pleasant lines and tanned the texture and color of brown leather; he wore out patiently and soon;—yet this art, in which he found delight, shows that he was a MAN,—not a slave!

This proof of spiritual quality so near to the heart of a people who have made a harmonious unit of their land and their life becomes daily more precious as our own pet commercial expedients sweep it forever into a past fast becoming dim—never to be reclaimed.[37]

That same year, in an unpublished essay prepared for Darwin D. Martin, Wright expounded further:

I went to Japan sufficiently alive to our sins and shortcomings as a material people. I came back believing the Japanese a truly spiritual people . . .

To contrast their pure and delicate art with the mass of Western art is to contrast the spiritual lines and exquisite grace of the single flower with the material richness of the much cultured rose: to contrast the symbol with the literal; the sensuous with the sensual; chastity and restraint with incontinence and gluttony . . . What makes a study of their civilization of special value to us is the great fact that the life of the Japanese is harmonious with . . . the heart of Nature.[38]

The Japanese, he said, were very poor, very simple and childhearted. In 1912 he wrote that the Japanese artist

is a true poet. Surely life in Old Japan must have been perpetual communion with the divine heart of Nature. For Nippon drew its racial inspiration from, and framed its civilization in accord with a native perception of Nature-law . . . Sympathy with Nature was spontaneous and inevitable.[39]

Wright's preoccupation with the natural beauty of Japan and the spirituality of its people has much to do with his own ethnic roots in the Driftless Area of southwest Wisconsin, with its rolling green hills and fantastic rock formations. Taliesin lies twenty miles from Richland

Center, the place of his birth in 1867. Most of his life was connected in some way to the land of his family, his own paradise (see Thomas H. Beeby, chapter 7 in this volume).

Recently Elisa Evett has argued convincingly that for the nineteenth-century critic "Japanese art seemed to embody a state of mind, a condition of being, and a quality of perception that was forever lost to the Western world."[40] Part of the European infatuation with Japan stemmed from the conviction that it was a pristine paradise of unrivaled natural beauty, populated with innocent, youthfully spirited people living in blissful harmony with their surroundings. The Japanese artist was depicted as a kind of Adam before the Fall, at one with himself and with nature, whereas European civilization was seen as old, effete, and worn out. Evett concluded that the

> primitivist sentiment aroused by Japan and its art is hardly surprising. Japan was an ideal prospect for those who had primitivist longings. It was a remote, exotic country, clouded in mystery by centuries of seclusion from the West, and thus rich in material for the imaginations of Westerners in search of fanciful escape from their pessimistic perceptions of the Western world. (Pp. 104–5)

The purity of Japanese culture seemed to be expressed most fully in the woodblock print, often described in the literature of the time as a primitive craft in the practice of which only the simplest tools and materials are used. One thinks of Gauguin and the "noble savages" he portrayed in the woodblock medium in Tahiti. Similarly, in 1887 Van Gogh portrayed Père Tanguy, the paint seller and cunning businessman, against a backdrop composed of ukiyo-e prints. Tanguy, wearing a rough jacket and his face bristling with a hard, grey beard, is transformed into the ideal of a simple Japanese tradesman who earned very little money. He is the man Van Gogh longed to be. "Here my life will become more and more like a Japanese painter's living close to nature like a petty tradesman," he wrote his brother from Arles in 1888. "If I can live long enough, I shall be something like old Tanguy."[41]

Van Gogh was rejected repeatedly in his own lifetime: first as a son by his hostile father, a minister with whom he had a very troubled relationship; then as a failed art dealer; and finally as a painter whose canvases could not be sold even by his younger brother, the successful art dealer on whom he was totally dependent financially. More than any of his counterparts, van Gogh needed and found confirmation of his own self-worth in Japanese art. Though he knew Japan only through Pierre Loti's *Madame Chrysanthème* and the flimsiest sheets of colored woodcuts, he saw in the prints what he longed for and what he wanted to see. By identifying himself so closely with Japan, he could set himself apart as an unusually sensitive connoisseur of a rarefied culture, a discerning initiate into special mysteries. And so it seems inevitable that he would take the final step and deliberately portray himself in the *Self-Portrait* of 1888, now in the Fogg Art Museum, with slanted eyes, close-shaven head, somber brown coat, and the halo effect of a Japanese monk worshipping the eternal Buddha.[42] Here he stands alone, but as the high priest of transcendent spiritual powers. His obsession with prints went far beyond that of his fellow artists. Van Gogh obviously needed this link with the Orient; it was surely a psychological as well as spiritual attraction.

A number of prominent westerners, dissatisfied with modern culture, were attracted to Japan in the late nineteenth century. Most intriguing for us is the wealthy Boston bachelor, William Sturgis Bigelow (1850–1926), remembered (if at all) as an eccentric dilettante who in 1911 donated a vast collection of Japanese art to Boston's Museum of Fine Arts, of which he was a trustee. In *No Place of Grace*, T. J. Jackson Lears characterizes the restless Bigelow as a sensitive, troubled man suffering from intense guilt and paralysis of the will occasioned by his inability to live up to the unreasonable goals set by his authoritarian father, a famous surgeon at Massachusetts General Hospital and Harvard Medical School. The son had studied bacteriology with Pasteur in Paris but was forced into a career in surgery by his father, a conflict that shaped the rest of his life, rendering him in effect a lifelong nervous invalid. Lears wrote that the young Bigelow

> could not sustain the tension between the duty of filial loyalty and the desire for professional self-esteem. He had to leave the medical profession to preserve some sense of his own worth. Yet ultimately he preserved very little. Judging by Bigelow's subsequent

FRANK LLOYD WRIGHT'S OTHER PASSION

6.16. William Sturgis Bigelow (1850–1926) in Japan in the 1880s. Photo, Courtesy, Museum of Fine Arts, Boston.

behavior, I would suggest that his repressed feelings of rebelliousness against paternal authority generated a sense of guilt, which turned his rage against himself. After his confrontation with his father, Bigelow became a lifelong nervous invalid. His protracted depressions and his persistent hypochondria served a dual purpose: they were rationalizations for his escape from the achievement ethos; they were also self-inflicted punishments for his failure to meet ego ideals. Lacking sufficient ego strength to chart his own course in bacteriology, Bigelow could only disengage himself, and drift.

During the winter of 1881–2, the drifting stopped for a time. At the Lowell Institute in Boston, Edward S. Morse gave a series of lectures on Japan, and Bigelow was captivated. By May 1882, he had arranged to join Morse on his return voyage to the Orient. In retrospect, Bigelow called the decision "the turning point of my life." It temporarily ended the long period of depression and aimlessness; it promised escape from the tension between autonomy and dependence.[43]

Depressive withdrawal and self-hatred propelled his rebellious flight in 1882 to Japan, where he lived for seven years in relative peace of mind, embarking on a serious and satisfying Buddhist pilgrimage, foreign to his American experience: "In embracing esoteric Buddhism," writes Lears, "Bigelow preserved his dependent role by leaving a stern father for a benign Ajari. The Ajari embodied paternal wisdom and maternal solace; he symbolically unified Bigelow's ideal father and his lost mother" (p. 229). Bigelow had himself photographed in Japan in the full regalia of a Buddhist pilgrim, a portrait that is as touching as it is humorous (fig. 6.16). His family fortune allowed him to collect Japanese art in overwhelming quantities, and he did so with an enlightened breadth of vision that encompassed all fields ranging from Buddhist paintings to sword guards; the ukiyo-e prints alone numbered a staggering 40,000.

Frank Lloyd Wright, of course, was another who found solace in the Orient. Throughout his life he surrounded himself with oriental art. Photographs of Taliesin interiors over the years reveal Chinese rugs on

FRANK LLOYD WRIGHT'S OTHER PASSION

6.17. Studio, Taliesin, Spring Green, ca. 1940–50. Photograph by Henry Fuermann. Courtesy of The Frank Lloyd Wright Memorial Foundation. The Buddhist objects above the mantle, from left to right, are a Chinese Buddha head, a seated Japanese wooden thousand-armed Kannon, and a Japanese triptych depicting the descent of the Buddha Amida and his heavenly host. The architectural models are for the Abraham Lincoln Center on the left and The San Francisco Call (The Press Building) on the right.

the floor and Chinese embroideries covering the tables. There were Japanese straw baskets, Japanese folding screens set into the walls, Japanese and Chinese ceramics displayed as decorative accents on ledges and, of course, ukiyo-e prints set out on specially designed stands (fig. 6.17). Particularly revealing, however, is the prevalence of Buddhist paintings and sculpture, often close to the hearth, the symbolic household altar.

The owners of oriental art galleries in New York can recall annual visits and substantial purchases by Wright even during the last fifteen years of his life when he was working on the Guggenheim Museum commission. He died owing money to at least one Japanese art dealer in New York. Further, it is well known that he continued to make use of his print collection as house gifts to clients, and as Christmas presents for his Taliesin Fellows.[44] The gift of a print to a client or special friend must have taken on symbolic value for him.

As a champion of democratic art, Wright was moved to praise woodcuts as the humble art of the people, and his preconceptions about Japanese art led him to describe prints in terms of the noble values he espoused as his own—spirituality, purity, and harmony with nature. While many things helped to distinguish Wright as a man of culture—his love of music and theatre spring to mind at once—it was oriental art and especially Japanese prints, which he always touted as "extremely rare" or "unique," that confirmed his self-image as a genius, a man of truly superior insight and refinement.

NOTES

The author wishes to acknowledge a debt of gratitude to Harold C. Price; Bruce Brooks Pfeiffer, Director of Archives, The Frank Lloyd Wright Memorial Foundation; William Wesley Peters, Chairman of the Board of the Frank Lloyd Wright Foundation and Taliesin Associated Architects; Edgar Tafel; Curtis Besinger; Stephen Addiss, The University of Kansas; David DeLong, The University of Pennsylvania; Sandy Kita, The University of Wisconsin-Madison; Roger Keyes; Endo Mitsumasa, Imperial Hotel; Edgar Kaufmann, Jr.; Kathryn Smith; David Kiehl, The Metropolitan Museum of Art; Scott Elliott, The Kelmscott Gallery; Shonnie Finnegan, State University of New York at Buffalo; Joseph Seo; Allan Chait; Robert D. Jacobsen, The Minneapolis Institute of Arts.

In this paper Japanese names appear in the traditional East Asian manner with family name first.

1. Letter from Frank Lloyd Wright to S. C. Bosch Reitz, 17 October 1922. Archives of The Metropolitan Museum of Art.

2. Frank Lloyd Wright, *An Autobiography* (London: Longmans, Green and Co., 1932), 204.

3. Geneviève Aitken and Marianne Delafond, *La Collection d'Estampes Japonaises de Claude Monet à Giverny* (Paris: La Bibliotheque des Arts, 1983).

4. For more on this subject, see Julia Meech-Pekarik, "Early Collectors of Japanese Prints and The Metropolitan Museum of Art," *Metropolitan Museum Journal* 17 (1984): 93–118.

5. Howard Mansfield, "Japenese Prints," *Transactions of the Grolier Club of the City of New York* (1899): 126, 128.

6. Frederick C. Moffatt, *Arthur Wesley Dow (1857–1922)* (Washington, D.C.: Smithsonian Institution Press, 1977), 70–75.

7. Shugio Hiromichi, *Catalogue of an Exhibition of Japanese Prints* (New York, 1896).

8. William Green, "A Peerless Pair: Frederick W. Gookin and Frank Lloyd Wright and the Art Institute of Chicago's 1908 Exhibition of Japanese Prints," *Andon* 14 (Summer 1984): 14–19.

9. Frank Lloyd Wright, *An Autobiography* (New York: Horizon Press, 1977), p. 217.

10. The album is in the collection of the Frank Lloyd Wright Home and Studio Foundation, Oak Park, Illinois.

11. Letter from Edwin H. Hewitt to Frank Lloyd Wright, June 20, 1908. Archives of The Minneapolis Institute of Arts.

12. Frank Lloyd Wright, *Antique Colour Prints from the Collection of Frank Lloyd Wright* (Chicago: The Arts Club of Chicago, 1917), 3.

13. Carol Shankel, *Sallie Casey Thayer and Her Collection* (Lawrence, Kansas: The University of Kansas Museum of Art, 1976), 26.

14. Wright-Martin Papers (MS 22.8), University Archives, State University of New York at Buffalo. Copyright © The Frank Lloyd Wright Foundation 1987. Courtesy of The Frank Lloyd Wright Memorial Foundation.

15. Wright often designed dresses for his wife and clients. See David A. Hanks, *The Decorative Designs of Frank Lloyd Wright* (New York: E. P. Dutton, 1979), 24–26.

16. Julia Meech-Pekarik, "Frank Lloyd Wright and Japanese Prints," *Metropolitan Museum of Art Bulletin* 40, no. 2 (Fall 1982): 52.

17. Wright, *An Autobiography* (1977), 551.

18. For the Metropolitan purchase see Meech-Pekarik, "Early Collectors of Japanese Prints," 111–12.

19. Kathryn Smith, "Frank Lloyd Wright and the Imperial Hotel: A Postscript," *The Art Bulletin* 68, no. 2 (June 1985): 297.

20. Quoted in ibid, 298. Copyright © The Frank Lloyd Wright Foundation 1985. Courtesy of the Frank Lloyd Wright Memorial Foundation. Emperor Meiji died in July 1912.

21. Wright, *An Autobiography* (1932), 204.

22. Wright, *An Autobiography* (1977), 554.

23. Meech-Pekarik, "Early Collectors of Japanese Prints," 107–9.

24. Wright, *An Autobiography* (1977), 550.

25. Wright, *Antique Colour Prints,* 1.

26. Meech-Pekarik, "Frank Lloyd Wright and Japanese Prints," 54–56.

27. David Waterhouse, *Images of Eighteenth-Century Japan* (Toronto: Royal Ontario Museum, 1975), 15.

28. Wright, *An Autobiography* (1977), 554–57.

29. Julia Meech-Pekarik, *Frank Lloyd Wright and Japanese Prints: The Collection of Mrs. Avery Coonley* (Washington, D.C.: American Institute of Architects, 1983).

30. Mark H. Ingraham, "The Van Vlecks: A Family of Intellect and Taste," *The Wisconsin Alumnus* (March–April 1981): 16–19.

31. Letter from Curtis Besinger to the author, 10 March 1985.

32. Transcript of Wright's print party talk on 20 September 1950. Copyright © The Frank Lloyd Wright Foundation 1982. Courtesy of The Frank Lloyd Wright Memorial Foundation.

33. Wright, *An Autobiography* (1977), 228.

34. Letter from William Wesley Peters to the author, 25 February 1985.

35. Narciso G. Menocal, "Form and Content in Frank Lloyd Wright's *Tree of Life* Window," *Elvehjem Museum of Art Bulletin* (1983–84): 26, 31, n. 26.

36. Wright, *An Autobiography* (1977), 217.

37. Frank Lloyd Wright, *Hiroshige: An Exhibition of Colour Prints from the Collection of Frank Lloyd Wright* (Chicago: The Art Institute of Chicago, 1906), 1–2.

38. This unpublished essay was an enclosure with a letter from Wright to Darwin D. Martin dated 11 August 1906. Wright-Martin Papers (MS 22.8), University Archives, State University of New York at Buffalo. Copyright © The Frank Lloyd Wright Foundation 1987. Courtesy of The Frank Lloyd Wright Memorial Foundation.

39. Frank Lloyd Wright, *The Japanese Print: An Interpretation* (Chicago: The Ralph Fletcher Seymour Co., 1912), 13.

40. Elisa Evett, "The Late Nineteenth-Century European Response to Japanese Art: Primitivist Leanings," *Art History* 6, no. 1 (March 1983): 104.

41. Vincent Van Gogh, *The Complete Letters of Vincent Van Gogh,* 3 vols. (Greenwich, Conn.: New York Graphic Society, 1958), 3:47.

42. Ibid., 64, 67.

43. T. J. Jackson Lears, *No Place of Grace: Antimodernism and the Transformation of American Culture 1880–1920.* (New York: Parthenon Books, 1981), 228.

44. See Edgar Tafel, *Apprentice to Genius* (New York: McGraw-Hill, 1979).

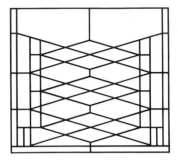

WRIGHT AND LANDSCAPE:
A MYTHICAL INTERPRETATION

7

THOMAS H. BEEBY

It is commonly held that the buildings of Frank Lloyd Wright fuse with their specific sites and demonstrate an organic link with the forces of nature. Wright himself suggests that the forms of the landscape are mysteriously related to the configuration of his buildings. The Prairie Houses, however, display an internal consistency between buildings, regardless of location, that suggests another interpretation lying outside of local site conditions. If there is a direct link between landscape and built form, it exists in a mythic terrain somewhere within the mind of the architect.

Taliesin, where Frank Lloyd Wright was buried in 1959, lies twenty miles from Richland Center, the place of his birth in 1867. Most of his life he was connected in some way to the land of his family in southwest Wisconsin. An argument could be constructed that calls for an ideal landscape as a basis for Wright's buildings; that is, a paradise or place of origin drawn from this beloved country that he knew so intimately from childhood.

The desire to return to nature for inspiration was a poetic preoccupation from romanticism, through the nineteenth century into the modern period (fig. 7.1). Returning to nature involves a nostalgia for paradise, for a reinstatement of the condition that existed at the beginning of all things. Knowing origins requires understanding the authentic history or myth of creation. Myth as defined by Mircea Eliade "narrates a sacred history; it relates an event that took place in primordial

Time, the fabled time of beginnings. In other words, myth tells how, through the deeds of Supernatural Beings a reality came into existence, be it the whole of reality, the Cosmos, or only a fragment of reality" (*Myth and Reality,* New York: Harper & Row, 1963, p. 5). A mythical account of the origin of the world is the supreme act of creation. It becomes the exemplar for every other type of creation. The making of the landscape is a possible paradigm for the construction of a building.

The settlement of the prairie is often viewed as a mythical account of the origin of the world, the establishment of a new reality by ancestors of supernatural proportion. Establishing a home on the frontier requires pragmatic choices about location, but it also involves selecting a special place that becomes a sanctuary for the family against the wilderness. The myths, legends, and rituals of the settlers consecrate the chosen place as being separate and discontinuous from the surrounding space that remains uncivilized and therefore in a state of chaos. Natural forms of the landscape reveal cosmic reality, become an incarnation of visions and dreams that are then coupled with concentrated cultural history. The relationship between those who toil on the earth and nature has changed very little since the beginning of agriculture. Nature is charged with mythic power in the animistic imagination of farmers and herdsmen. The ground is broken, the seed planted, and the necessary rituals are performed to placate the spirits of the place.

The first thing done in a new land is to name the elements of the landscape, for a place with no name is intimidating. The pioneer brings names with him as well as attached memories and cultural associations. The hills of Wright's childhood all had Welsh names. Spring Green was a designation chosen by others to honor the first grass that sprouted on the southern slopes, facing the Wisconsin River, while the rest of the world was still gripped by winter.

As a child, Frank Lloyd Wright wandered his family's farm in Spring Green; later he spent his summers working on the land with his relatives. There is a period in a child's life, prior to adolescence, when the natural world is perceived in an educational way. The processes of nature and an empathy with natural forms become an indelible memory of the world. Early perceptual continuity with the landscape and its

7.1.   Under the overhanging rock. Photo by Henry Hamilton Bennett. Reproduced courtesy of The H. H. Bennett Studio of Wisconsin Dells, Wisconsin.

formation remains as a basis for intuition. Genius insures the intensity and accessibility of this understanding. The paradise of childhood remains forever an active component of adult memory.

Paradise for Frank Lloyd Wright existed within the "Driftless Area" of Wisconsin. The name derives from the fact that this region miraculously was saved from glacial destruction and residual drift. As the glacier of the Wisconsin Ice Sheet pushed south from the Arctic, it ground to a halt against the Baraboo Hills, split in half to later rejoin south of the Driftless Area. At the end of this final glacial period, the receding ice melted, forming a vast lake that drained down the Wisconsin River. The flood created an immense valley of sand bars enclosed by rock bluffs (fig. 7.2). The fantastic rock formations found in the vicinity of the Wisconsin Dells is evidence of the power of this flow and was captured in

WRIGHT AND LANDSCAPE

UNDER THE OVERHANGING ROCK, WISCONSIN DELLS
Copyright 1896, by H. H. Bennett

early photographs by H. H. Bennett, who understood the poetic power of the processes of nature.

The ancient landscape of the Driftless Area was formed by milleniums of weathering. Its worn face is turned up to the infinity of the sky. The vault of heaven, azure blue and transcendent, spreads over the recumbent body of the earth. The sky is home of the masculine celestial divinities that fertilize the receptive body of the earth. Planets course through the heavens, ordering all life below. The sun rises from the underworld each dawn. It has always been a symbol of heroes sent to save the world from destruction. The bull is the primary symbol of the fertile power of the sun. Burning across the sky, the sun's energy gives life to all; however, it can also destroy those not protected from its searing force. At the end of each day the sun dies to return to the

7.2.   High Rock from Romance
Cliff. Photo by Henry Hamilton
Bennett. Reproduced courtesy
of The H. H. Bennett Studio of
Wisconsin Dells, Wisconsin.

underworld. In its absence, the darkened sky is illuminated by the light
of millions of stars suddenly made visible in the reflected glow emanat-
ing from the underworld.

The moon, tragic orb of twilight, governs the night sky. The everchanging female presence of the moon waxes and wanes, disappearing
each month for three days of ritual death. All cyclical phenomena such
as the movement of the waters, growth of vegetation, and fertility of
animal life are governed by the moon. Time is measured by the span of
each lunar cycle. Tied closely to women and the earth; life, death, and
resurrection are also within the changing domain of lunar control. The
spirits of the restless dead dance in the moonbeams, while the souls of
the blessed rise to escape on the moon. Snakes, owls, cicada, and

WRIGHT AND LANDSCAPE

7.3. Artist's Glen. Photo by Henry Hamilton Bennett. Reproduced courtesy of The H. H. Bennett Studio of Wisconsin Dells, Wisconsin.

creatures of change such as the frog represent lunar presence on earth.

The wrath of the divinities of the sky is expressed in the overwhelming power of the weather. The wind, constantly moving over the body of the earth diminishes her surface. Freezing blasts from the north advance each year to destroy all life that is not sheltered from their devastating power. Clouds gather in summer skies to unleash the thunder and lightning that roars and flashes over the land. The rain from the

heavens falls on the land, giving life, while also removing its substance, grain by grain. Water gathers into rivulets, joins into streams, and finally flows in great rivers toward the sea. In an ancient land such as the Driftless Area, the forms of the rises are low and rounded. The valleys are steep and tortuous. It is a region of dissected tableland with broad ridges of limestone separated widely by poorly drained valley floors (fig. 7.3). These deep and winding spaces are sharply delineated by exposed rock escarpments (fig. 7.4). Alternate layers of limestone and sandstone are eroded differentially, creating figural rock formations with deep overhangs, projecting ledges, and shallow caves. Erosion or carving by water exposes the stratification or structure of the earth. The undercut walls of the valleys appear as overhanging volumes that

WRIGHT AND LANDSCAPE

float over the shadowed surface of the rivers. Vertical rock formations are not constructed, they are the remains of solid material; ancient ruins of geological history (fig. 7.5). Eroded space created by water is a sinuously flowing fluid. Ever moving in increasing volume and decreasing speed, it gathers finally in limpid pools and vast flowages before spreading over the ocean, birthplace of all life.

Surface water seeps through the fissures in the rock. Moving in hidden streams, it carves labyrinthean caves of continuously linked chambers: the womb of the earth (fig. 7.6). The spatial development of caves follows the same pattern as surface erosion, for a cave is a valley within the earth. The material of the walls is seamless and runs continuously up to become the ceiling, as one monolithic surface. Space

WRIGHT AND LANDSCAPE   161

7.6.   Looking out from Phantom Chamber. Photo by Henry Hamilton Bennett. Reproduced courtesy of The H. H. Bennett Studio of Wisconsin Dells, Wisconsin.

flows from chamber to chamber, ever increasing in size. The configuration is an exact result of the speed and volume of the water and the quality of the stratum that it traverses. The caves occasionally open to the sky, creating a zone of perpetual twilight, familiar in myth as the aura of the Land of the Dead (fig. 7.7). Caves are often the dwelling places of deities and oracles of the underworld. A miraculous spring bubbles in their caves, and immersion in its water guarantees purification or spiritual rebirth. All life rises from water, it is the essence of fer-

WRIGHT AND LANDSCAPE

tility. The serpent slides out of the darkened cave each spring, shedding his skin to signal the return of life.

A legend of the Winnebago Indians relates the story of the creation of the Wisconsin River (fig. 7.8). A serpent leaving the northern forest slid south across the landscape leaving the winding trail of the river. Smaller side valleys are the traces of creatures fleeing to escape its jaws. The contorted rock formations are regions where the serpent had to squeeze through crevices, rubbing against the enclosing walls.

The inversion of the negative spatial component of the landscape, as if cast for a mold, is the positive form of the earth itself. The rounded hills of the Driftless Area stand as isolated mounds across the valleys. These hills are the body of the Earth Mother, who gives life to all things

WRIGHT AND LANDSCAPE   163

7.8.   The Navy Yard. Photo by
Henry Hamilton Bennett. Re-
produced courtesy of The H. H.
Bennett Studio of Wisconsin
Dells, Wisconsin.

and whose good will is necessary to insure bountiful harvests. The worship of the female deity of the earth is one of the oldest known religions that exists today in residual form. Her realm, closely related to the moon and darkness, includes not only the fertility of women and agriculture but also deals with the cycles of life and death. The penetration of her body by the plow and the planting of the seed risks her wrath and must be ritually controlled. Erotic magic surrounds the agricultural year when fertility must be insured for survival. The earth gives birth, feeds, and after death receives man back. Newborn children are lain on the body of the earth to draw sustenance, the sick are placed in furrows to recover, and the dead are buried in fetal positions waiting for rebirth.

The crests of the ancient hills in the Driftless Area frequently have

WRIGHT AND LANDSCAPE

7.9.   Tower through window at Chi-coon-grah (Parted Bluff). Photo by Henry Hamilton Bennett. Reproduced courtesy of The H. H. Bennett Studio of Wisconsin Dells, Wisconsin.

stone outcroppings as evidence of their age (fig. 7.9). Structures of colossal scale and evocative form, they appear to be man-made, the remains of a long-departed race. Stone is awe inspiring in its eternal presence that transcends life. Figural stones stand motionless, terrifying spectres from the forgotten past. Vertical stones are often used to mark the graves of those who died violently, their souls entering the stone to be eternally trapped. Silhouetted above the tops of the hills, seen against the sky as transcendent markers, they connect the three primary cosmic zones of experience. Extending from the underworld, they loom above the surface of the earth, reaching for the vault of heaven. Along their axis and through their substance courses the cosmic energy of the place, concentrated and made concrete.

Vegetation is mythically explained through the relationship of the

WRIGHT AND LANDSCAPE   165

earth to the sky. The male presence of the sky stretches over the receiving body of the earth, and from their union, a son is created who rules the kingdom of the plant world. Each winter he dies, only to be reborn with the coming of the next spring. Every year the appearance of new foliage is followed by flowering, fruit, and eventually death. The seed represents, in concentrated form, the entire potential of the world of vegetation. Flowers are cut and brought from the woods and meadows for ritual purposes. Certain fruits are eaten, others are forbidden, and the cutting of plants for their medicinal power is based on ancient practice.

The cycle of plant life is a symbol for man's existence on earth, and certain images have become central to his understanding of the world. The tree can be interpreted as a representation of man standing upright on the land exposed to the ravages of weather. A tree can also represent the entire cosmos. Bound into the body of the earth, the crown of the tree is part of the heavens. The trunk becomes a conduit that connects heaven and earth. A frequent association found in myth and legend is a tree growing next to a stone. An altar sheltered by the shade of the tree is indicated by the standing stone. This image of a sacred place is expanded to include sacred groves with groupings of stones. These sites are primitive sanctuaries that, until this day, have continued to be inhabited by a succession of religions.

The Driftless Area is a veritable Garden of Eden. The island saved from the glacier supplied the seed for the resurrection of the flora for the entire region. Because of the diversity of habitats, a larger number of plant communities exist here than in either the forest to the north or the prairie to the south. The soils affect the distribution of species within the landscape. The upper slopes are only covered with a thin mantle of soil, while the heavier loam lies in deep layers in the valleys. Because the Wisconsin River valley is the dividing line that separates forest from prairie, the landscape varied drastically throughout history. The surface of the land was completely forested in times of heavy rain; the grass dominated in periods of frequent droughts. The landscape of Wright's childhood can be reconstructed with reasonable accuracy.

A peninsula of relic, tall grass prairie extended north from Illinois to cross the Wisconsin River at Spring Green. Elsewhere a forest domi-

WRIGHT AND LANDSCAPE

nated by poplar and willow grew on the rich bottomland that flooded each spring. The poplar, traditionally the tree of despair, and the willow, long associated with witchcraft, grew in the dampness where soil and water mix. On slightly higher land, above the river but still under its influence, grew a dense forest of elm and maple with smaller trees such as ash and elder. Ash was used as a charm against the power of water and drowning. Elder was a fearsome plant that could cause sickness and death. Woody vines climbed over the trees, often attaining great size. Tangles of wild grape evoked images of the ecstatic rituals associated with its intoxicating fruit.

The hills above the river were wooded on the northern slopes with a forest of maple, basswood, and walnut. A clearly defined understory grew beneath the canopy of taller trees. This thicket included birch, hazel, and brambles and provided the tactile element of the woods. Birch, the tree that first shows green in spring, its branches were used to drive out evil and death. Hazelnuts contained the concentrated wisdom of nature. The brambles' fruit could only be eaten at certain times of the year. The southern slopes were prairie. Spreading up from the open valley below, the grass covered that portion of the hill that faced the sun. The hilltops were open grassland with groves of Burr Oak growing in isolated groupings, survivors of the prairie fires that burned each fall. Oak, the tree that courts the lightning bolt, symbolized the presence on earth of the celestial divinities. In heroic isolation, these trees stood like battered warriors in a sea of green. Finding shelter at the edge of the groves beneath their gnarled branches were hawthorns, the May trees of ancient spring rites.

The Prairie House is a mythical interpretation of the landscape of Frank Lloyd Wright's childhood brought to light through the adult memory of the architect. For Wright, the landscape was alive and inseparable from the natural history of the place. He wished to create a new life within the shelter of his houses. He had a nostalgia for paradise, for a time that preceded the architectural artifacts of his age. Through the rites of building he wanted to establish a new reality, giving life by possessing the cosmic power of nature. The earth was to relinquish her substance in order to construct the house, but more importantly, to infuse the construction with the power of the processes of nature. His intention was to establish a sanctuary that was part of the landscape, but necessarily an intensification of its composition. The settlement of his family's land by his grandfather elevated that particular place above the more mundane territory surrounding it. The elements of the landscape, as interpreted by his child's mind, became a paradigm that could be repeated endlessly, for it had mythical power in its origin. Through the necessary symbolism and geometry, the house becomes a container of spiritual power.

The Prairie House could be interpreted as a place of refuge, the equivalent of a special place that children seek to escape the oppression of the adult world. It is hidden in the landscape, concealed whenever physically possible from the surrounding built world. Appearing among the trees that always envelop the structure in Wright's drawings, the house merges visually with the site. The living room faces the line of approach, either the street or a natural opening in the trees. The mass of the structure is preceded by a series of horizontal platforms or gardens enclosed by low walls that mark off a precinct surrounding the house. The vertical surfaces of these horizontal features are normally masonry extending down into the earth. Sometimes constructed of stone, these walls are laid up in a manner suggesting natural limestone shelving. When constructed of brick, the horizontal joints are raked to resemble the character of natural stone. When these walls have a surface that is monolithic material, such as concrete or stucco, horizontal trim is introduced to ensure stratification that follows the surface of the land. In every case, the contact with the earth is made with a stone or concrete base that projects slightly, suggesting a natural rise in the bedrock to support the weight of the building. This type of formation is approximated at the base of the hills in the Driftless Area where flooding has exposed stone ledges that project through the topsoil.

Standing on this base are the walls that contain the space within the house. Constructed of the same material as the base, the walls rise up to but seldom touch the underside of the roof. Stone piers lift from the earth, projected in front of the walls to visually support the roof volumes. Freestanding masonry masses of varying heights radiate from the center of the structure, decreasing in height as they increase in distance from the focus of the composition. These vertical elements evoke the eroded pillars of stone that line the Wisconsin River valley. Behind them, the walls of the house represent the bluffs with their scoured surfaces worn by the action of the river water. A continuous void that is perpetually in shadow flows above these enclosing walls. The glass is frequently deeply recessed, further implying the carving of water into the body of the structure. This is an exact image of the condition in the landscape where a limestone shelf projects over an eroded sandstone depression. The large openings that occur in major rooms are often buttressed by massive masonry piers. Intermediate wood supports between windows and doors are stained dark to resemble tree trunks and support the volume of the roof, representing the canopy of leaves in a grove.

The structures of the roofs are generally hipped and low in profile. Wood shingles or tiles form a textured volume that could be interpreted to be the slopes of the mounds of the Driftless Area. Extending out into the site in a centrifugal manner, the roofs imply the natural configuration of ancient linear hills merging above the deep valleys. At the center or crossing of the roofs projects the masonry core of the chimney, like a stone outcropping isolated by weathering above the eroded surface of a hill. The central masonry stack of the chimney combines with the surrounding masonry pillars to confirm the notion that this is an ancient sanctuary, signified by vertical stone outcroppings. At its center is the altar where the ritual household fire is burned. Plants and vines grow on the ledges below the roofs. Gardens surround the house, drawing it into the landscape. Existing trees are incorporated into the composition in a manner that suggests that the house is part of the landscape and has always inhabited this site since the origin of the place.

The house must be approached carefully, for it does not reveal itself to the casual observer. The point of entry is concealed. Sometimes a reflecting pond lies before the main living spaces, indicating the presence of the river in the mind of Wright, shining beneath the hills, reflecting rippled light up onto the darkened bluffs. Circling the face of the house, the approach passes between masonry outcroppings. It is like traversing the landscape down a winding hollow before climbing up a hillside. Entry is an initiation, for this is a haven from the chaos of the surroundings. The house is a labyrinth with a protected center. The portal, sometimes an arch like a cave opening, designates the threshold, the point of final initiation. The entry chamber is compressed, often leading to winding stairs that climb up to the main spaces.

The Prairie House displays a spatial sensibility in its formation that closely resembles the erosive forces of water that carved the Driftless Area. From the smaller chambers in the extremities of the house, the space flows in tortuous channels toward the main living area. Openings to the exterior are limited, primarily to a high clerestory void in secondary areas. The high sidewall of this enclosure acts like a dam, restricting horizontal movement of interior space. The spatial flow, once it reaches the primary zone, is dissipated in the higher volumes of these rooms. The space slows and fills the void, carving ample chambers, and eventually floods out through controlled openings into the site. The entire house is conceived as an arrangement that resembles a river valley in its containment.

The tree cover in the Driftless Area occurs on the northern slopes of the hills, protected from the sun. The prairie opens up the south side of the hill creating long vistas. The disposition of light and space within a Prairie House is similar. Ideally the living room opens to the south, or on a constricted site, the living room faces an ample lawn fronting on the open channel of the street. The rear of the house becomes the equivalent of the forest on the northern slopes of the hills. The trees are brought up against the structure, openings are severely limited, and the deep overhangs reduce the level of light to approximate the illumination in a deep forest.

The dim light of the interior also suggests the perpetual twilight of the underworld or that of a shallow cave. The entire arrangement heightens this sense, for the continuous flow of space is detailed to accentuate the horizontality of the surfaces, evoking the stratification of the rock walls of a cave formed by erosion. The continuity of finish between wall and ceiling approaches the monolithic material distribution familiar in caves. This illusion is further heightened by the rising slope of the ceiling planes toward the center of the rooms. The overall impression is that of the sheltering confines of the prenatal condition of the womb that is symbolized by the void of a cave.

The house is lifted out of the dampness of the earth, with the living areas on the second level. This allows views from the house above the ornamental plantings of the understory and through the open tree trunks, passing below the canopy of leaves overhead. The experience of entry is the equivalent of climbing above the thicket that grows along the river's edge, escaping the brambles and insects, to catch the breeze and look down on the smothering lushness of the valley. The plants growing on the ledges along the house bring to mind the vines growing among the trees and provide the sense of being hidden in a secret overlook, buried in vegetation. The space on the exterior that is formed between the understory and the forest canopy is carried inside the house through the vertical mullions that signify tree trunks and the linear trim that defines the interior space of the house. The glazing is broken down into ornamental leaded casements that obscure vision. Colored glass patterns represent the leaves and flowers of the shrubbery that is found at the edge of a forest or grove where the added light there creates a wall of foliage. Skylights are also cut through the ceiling volumes allowing filtered sunlight to flicker into the hollow of the house. The entire structure becomes a grove surrounding the masonry altar of the hearth. The canopy of trees protects its initiates from the burning sun and devasting winds of the prairie, where there is no shelter from nature.

The fireplace is the geometric and symbolic center of the house, for here is where the sacred flame of the family is kept burning. The oak logs are offered, the smoke rises into the sky. The flame is enclosed in a massive masonry core that is often ornamented profusely. This pillar, weighing so heavily on the earth, displaces the roof structure and ascends into the sky. Connecting the vault of heaven with the underworld, the conduit opens into the dwelling of man to warm and sustain him with fire. It is the cosmic center of the house where all the forces of the landscape are concentrated. The hearth faces the major opening or outfall to the site. The space of the entire house flows across its face before running out into the world.

The interior of the house is held in shadow. The colors are the full yet somber tones of autumn, the time of harvest. Branches of trees, flowers, and gathered weeds are placed in vessels throughout the house. The bounty of nature is used in ritual decoration. The same law that governs the distribution of form in nature governs the placement of elements in the house. Growing from a central stem, the chimney, the wood trim runs continuously throughout the house in constant horizontal lines. Over the windows and along the floor, connecting with all the vertical mullions, the trim draws the house into a system of natural growth as one heroic tree. Through division and subdivision, the interior is woven into a pattern resembling the unfolding of a plant from stem, to branch, to twig, to leaf and flower. Natural materials are lovingly presented as finishes throughout the house. The walls and ceilings of exposed sand plaster, in its natural hue, is the color and substance of the sandbars that line the Wisconsin River. The smooth oak trim is taken from the groves of the prairie. Stone is quarried from the earth and stacked to resemble nature. Clay is fired and used as a substitute for stone, as is concrete. The oak floors are covered with heavy rugs with abstracted leaf patterns, approximating the forest floor covered with a soft layer of dead leaves and small flowering plants that grow in the rich compost of decaying matter. Ornamental surface patterns of tile reflect the everchanging ripple of light glittering through the leaded casements.

The house becomes a poem to the bounty of the earth. A spiritual haven that encompasses the sacred altar of the family, marked by the pillars of masonry, it lies within the protecting body of the earth. The canopy of the sacred grove stretches overhead creating a womb or cave that protects and nurtures man within the landscape. He is not allowed to rise above the cave within the mound or to experience communication with heaven. The weight of the roof volumes bind the initiate to the earth: his beginning and eventual destiny. The poetics of the space attract and repel at once, for the question remains to be answered: Is this the security that precedes birth or the final resting place of death? Here we are returned to our origins; it is a realizable eternity. We can look out on the landscape and feel at one with its creative processes.

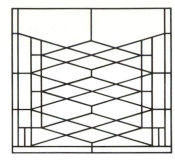

THE PRAIRIE IN LITERARY CULTURE AND THE PRAIRIE STYLE OF FRANK LLOYD WRIGHT

LARZER ZIFF

8

My dear and honored Walt Whitman," Louis Sullivan began the letter of February 3, 1887, in which he introduced himself to the poet. When he read *Leaves of Grass,* he told him, "you then and there entered my soul, have not departed, and will never depart."[1] The democratic faith of Whitman, it seemed, would be justified by the art of the Midwest where it could be embodied, free of the older patterns of the colonial past from which popular democracy was never quite separate on the Atlantic seaboard. So great was Whitman's influence on Sullivan's ideas that in his study of Sullivan Sherman Paul felt it appropriate to head his chapters with titles taken from Whitman: "Starting from Paumanok"; "Democratic Vistas"; "A Backward Glance."

But although Frank Lloyd Wright also admired the Whitman of democratic optimism and organic style directly as well as, it may be assumed, reflexively during his fruitful association with Sullivan, it would not be good judgment to parallel his career with epigraphs from *Leaves of Grass.* Despite his genealogical credentials from New England and some childhood years spent there, Wright springs undeniably from Wisconsin. When the poetic mood is on his prose, as it frequently is, it is the mood of the Welsh bards rather than of Whitman. Like those of the Celtic chanters, the exhortations in Wright's prose are also dappled with obscurities. The play of light and shade is not confined to his buildings.

Yet Whitman does supply the most striking similarity that American literature affords to Wright's work. Although it is not my intention to center on parallels between literature and architecture—a subject beyond my knowledge and also, I suspect, one that is vulnerable to all sorts of well-meant misrepresentations—before I come to my central concern, that of the literary perception of the prairies against which Wright's Prairie style asserted itself, some sense of Whitman will not be amiss. Whatever his specific influence may have been in the latter decades of nineteenth-century America, Whitman's was the only literary voice that insisted that the opportunity which the American West once symbolized—the establishment of the community of democratic brotherhood—was still possible to realize despite the setbacks of the Civil War, the rise of caste if not classes in an industrializing society, and the corruption of political processes by the pirates of finance. Henry James chose to focus on Americans only after they had emerged from native ground onto a finer soil, and Mark Twain saw them, increasingly saw all mankind, as different in kind from the truths they proclaimed. But Whitman took them for the promise they represented.

If Whitman alone sounded the optimistic note convincingly, it was because of the way he said what he said, not because of the message itself. The truth he proclaimed was validated not by the facts—he spoke a good deal about promises rather than fulfillment—but by his demonstration. If America represented the arrival of new values—the death of hierarchy and the establishment of the dignity of the common man—then it represented also the death of the old art forms and the arrival of new forms generated by the new values.

> I harbor for good or bad, I permit to speak at every hazard,
> Nature without check with original energy,

Whitman announced in his first masterpiece,[2] signifying that he wished to bring into consciousness the great primal resource which underlay all life and art but which traditional art had formalized out of existence. He did not, therefore, offer poems, but promised his reader that if he stopped with the poet he would "possess the origin of all poems" (l. 33). To read the words of *Leaves of Grass* was to be enabled rather than informed, to become a poet rather than to remain an audience.

Whitman thus attempted to move Americans out from the delusions which had arisen from cultures that denied the democratic principle and to locate them in a radical awareness of the reality they inhabited. In the process, his imagery characteristically associated buildings with dead forms and the out-of-doors with American reality:

> Houses and rooms are full of perfumes, the shelves are crowded
>   with perfumes,
> I breathe the fragrance myself and know it and like it,
> The distillation would intoxicate me also, but I shall not let it.
>
> The atmosphere is not a perfume, it has no taste of the
>   distillation, it is odorless,
> It is for my mouth forever, I am in love with it,
> I will go to the bank by the wood and become undisguised and
>   naked,
> I am mad for it to be in contact with me. (ll. 14–20)

It is tempting, treacherously so, to label this manner organic. Certainly in the presence of Whitman's poems we feel that the spill of words, which visually defy margins and refuse to arrange themselves in the black-and-white architecture of the sonnet or the heroic couplet, represents the striving of meaning to find signifiers and of signifiers to extend themselves to whatever shape is necessary for them to arrive at full signification. But beyond this, questions arise which trouble the simple notion of organic. Is the written word not different in kind from the spoken? Are the seemingly artificial forms in which poetry is arranged inorganic if they assist the signifier to signify? In the light of such questions, it is prudent to suggest that what Whitman liked to call his swimming shapes also have their form, a form which in its seeming formlessness may be called the convention of the organic, just as Mark Twain's colloquial style may be called the convention of the colloquial, actual talk being far more repetitious and inconsequential than the literary similitude he constructs to stand for it.[3]

Still, the impulse that propels Whitman is a pulse that throbbed in the American Romantic period, but which he alone maintained toward century's end. In 1852, for example, three years before the first edition of *Leaves of Grass,* the Yankee sculptor Horatio Greenough published his manifesto:

By beauty I mean the promise of function.
By action I mean the presence of function.
By character I mean the record of function.[4]

Yet in response to whatever constraints, Greenough himself sculpted Washington in a toga, engaged, that is, in what a disappointed Emerson called a futile endeavor to revive dead forms.[5] Whitman, however, frankly and fully acknowledged a social function for his poetry and throughout the century continued to be a symbol—an increasingly lone one as decades passed—of the coherence of nature, democracy, the United States, and a new art.

The idea of the American West was central to this faith. There was, all agreed, something more American about the West. "The damned shadow of Europe," as Hawthorne called it,[6] had not fallen over the plains, and from that region, it was to be expected, democracy's true voice would speak through an art which took its clues from limitless space and the voice of nature speaking from its midst, unfiltered by human conventions. Yet while writers spoke often of the westerners who were destined to fulfill the promise of the nation, the great works of the 1850s were neither by westerners nor about the West, except as it stood on the margin as a place in the imagination. Emerson, Thoreau, Hawthorne, and Melville were centered elsewhere even when they departed from the literal settings of their native regions. Whitman's celebration of the outdoors insofar as it invoked the plains was just that, an invocation of a rising region of the mind rather than a rendering of the life that was taking shape on it.

This is hardly surprising since the plains were not yet settled and so furnished scant material for arts dependent upon lived life and the social values that emerged from it. And yet it is remarkable because in the period immediately prior to the great outburst of literary creativity in the 1850s, when Cooper, Bryant, and Irving occupied the stage as America's three most distinguished men of letters, the prairies were such a powerful presence in the culture that each of them not only wrote about them but even titled a major work after them. In 1827 Cooper published his novel *The Prairie;* in 1833 Bryant published his poem "The Prairies"; and in 1835 Irving published his narrative *A Tour*

THE PRAIRIE STYLE OF FRANK LLOYD WRIGHT

on the Prairies. The absence of similar attention among the next generation of writers, therefore, is not so much an indication of the prematurity of the subject as it is of a collapse of interest in it.

The word "prairie" first entered literary English when Sir Thomas Browne used it to describe the grassy savanna of Provence. The term crossed the Atlantic in 1778 when its first printed appearance was in application to the grasslands of Virginia. In 1787 it appeared in an English work concerned with the region we now call the prairies, doubtless prompted by the early penetration of that territory by the French from whom the word was taken. The word became increasingly common in English as the landscape it denoted came under the control of English-speaking America after the Louisiana Purchase of 1803. Political and economic curiosity ran high, and explorers' accounts soon sprang up to feed it. Not too long after, writers began the literary exploration of its cultural potential.

Bryant's 124-line poem, "The Prairies," is a model of the conventions that were adapted to encompass the new subject matter. It begins:

> These are the gardens of the Desert, these
> The unshorn fields, boundless and beautiful,
> For which the speech of England has no name—
> The Prairies.[7]

The originality of the challenge they present to the imagination is most immediately signaled by the observation that England—not English—has no name for them; the very term in English is uniquely American. The more precise nature of their uniqueness as well as the way in which that uniqueness is to be comprehended imaginatively is captured in a phrase which was to reecho through the century, "gardens of the Desert," an oxymoron of controlled growth and emptiness, human endeavor and divine creation, which is rephrased throughout the poem, as in the term "verdant Waste" (l. 35) in the following stanza.

The thrust of Bryant's contemplation of this awesome phenomenon is to reduce it to human scale without trivializing its wondrous features. Although the prairies possess characteristics conventionally associated in aesthetics with the sublime—they are like the ocean; man has no part in the glorious work but they come directly from God's hand—Bryant resists the upward movement toward the sublime and works to comprehend his subject within the less rarefied category of the beautiful. So, for example, after seeing the prairie as a fitting floor for the magnificent temple of the sky, with flowers "whose glory and whose multitude / Rival the constellations!" (ll. 29–30), he checks the rise toward pure awe and curves it downward to a human scale:

> The great heavens
> Seem to stoop down upon the scene in love,—
> A nearer vault, and of a tenderer blue,
> Than that which bends above our Eastern hills. (ll. 31–34)

That downward curve initiates the next movement of the poem, which is a consideration of the prairies as the scene of a social life that is now extinct. Taking up the popular notion that the Mound Builders whose barrows yet stood were a people separate from the North American Indians of his day racially as well as chronologically, he paints a picture of the prairies' past when an agricultural people harvested their crops, tamed the bison to the yoke, and

> Heaped with long toil, the earth, while yet the Greek
> Was hewing the Pentelicus to forms
> Of symmetry, and rearing on the rock
> The glittering Parthenon. (ll. 47–50)

A "forgotten language" (l. 56) had once domesticated the desert, and the verdant waste the poet now beholds is not, after all, primal, but a second growth, the mighty grave of a cultured people overwhelmed and annihilated by the "warlike and fierce" (l. 59) red man. The prairie wolf and the gopher, like the Indian, are not original occupants of the scene, and the waste is humanized by its dead and fertilized to yield another social harvest. The poem's closing, then, can see the prairies which are now quick with the life of insects, flowers, and "gentle quadrupeds, / And birds," (ll. 105–6) as the inevitable site of another agricultural people, and the poet dreams of this:

From the ground,
Comes up the laugh of children, the soft voice
Of maidens, and the sweet and solemn hymns
Of Sabbath worshippers. The low of herds
Blends with the rustling of the heavy grain
Over the dark brown furrows. (ll. 117–22)

Different as his *Prairie* is from Bryant's "Prairies," Cooper neverthe-less shares with Bryant a concern with the literary strategy that will comprehend this unique phenomenon and a belief that that strategy is best developed in terms of the society that will live on the prairies, even though the period in which his fiction is set precedes such settle-ment. While Cooper is more given to stressing the sublimity of the va-cant wastes than Bryant, at the same time as a novelist he is in need of social life. So he cannot merely dream of the future but must, at the risk of losing all probability, introduce onto his prairies a cast of charac-ters who represent civilized society, in addition to the trapper and the Indians, even though fully half of the members of this assemblage have no real business being where he puts them. As a result, to the extent that he is open to the sublime he is also vulnerable to bathos.

Two remarkable death scenes close the novel, and while one may make the general observation that no literary convention is a trustier supplier of closure than death, still, in *The Prairie* the deaths assume a function peculiar to the problem of the setting itself. Bryant needed to feel the presence of the dead before he could comprehend the prairies as an appropriate site for the living. Cooper, eschewing the Mound Builders myth, leaves his scene as vacant of social life at the close as he had found it at the opening, save that it is marked by two graves. In one lies a man of mythic stature, the first white man to traverse the region, whose gifts blend the natural rhythms of the land to the sensibilities of civilization. In the other lies the first white man to commit willful murder on the prairie and that against a member of his family. Sym-bolic Adam and symbolic Cain provide the landmarks for the society to follow; without death there is no life.

As Henry Nash Smith has shown, Cooper's view of the West does advance significantly beyond that of his peers in one important respect.[8]

He introduces Ishmael Bush as representative of the class of rude husbandmen scarcely emerged from the hunter state who will first plow the prairies, and he employs him to symbolize the necessarily coarse life preliminary to culture. However, he uncovers in him a moral sublimity that is not to be attributed to the kind of refined sensibility his novels, including *The Prairie,* consistently assert to be the property of civilization and thus the justification for the conquest of the wild. Bush's power is primal. He embodies the notion that the prairies shape human culture to their own standard of unlicensed truth rather than exist in order to be shaped by socialized versions of truth. The notion is isolated in the character of Bush and is at war with the thematic values Cooper more explicitly maintains, but it remains as a buried message, available to those who will exhume it.[9] In the context of the 1830s, however, Ishmael Bush was an exception, a character who momentarily escaped from the restraints of the conscious mind. As his name indicated, he was to be read more conventionally as another formulation of the oxymoron governing the conceptualization of the prairies: Ishmael, a wanderer; Bush, a rooted plant.

"We send our youth abroad to grow luxurious and effeminate in Europe," Washington Irving wrote in his *Tour on the Prairies,* "it appears to me that a previous tour on the prairies would be more likely to produce that manliness, simplicity, and self-dependence most in unison with our political institutions."[10] His prairies are a finishing school which the civilized should attend, a reenforcer of a democratic culture but not its generator. Those who actually reside on the prairies are not as a result manly, simple, and self-dependent, but are characterized, rather, as a "rabble rout of nondescript beings that keep about the frontier between civilised and savage life; as those equivocal birds, the bats, hover about the confines of light and darkness" (p. 19). If we smile at the concluding pages of Irving's *Tour,* in which his party after a month's hunting sport on the prairies straggles back to the despised frontier in a condition so far from manly self-dependence that their survival depends upon their reaching a friendly farm before starvation overtakes them, the irony is lost on the author.

The prairies thus settled into the literary, which is to say the essentially eastern, imagination as a wild space awaiting a social life and a

THE PRAIRIE STYLE OF FRANK LLOYD WRIGHT

culture which would replicate the civilization of the Atlantic seaboard. Their appeal was greater in the promise than in the early realization, since the latter would for some while be marked by the nondescript beings of whom Irving wrote. Until the replication of the eastern town was accomplished, there was little to add to the tale told by Bryant, Cooper, and Irving. The writers of the remarkable generation which succeeded theirs focused on other matters. Left to the popular imagination, the prairies were pictured as the opposite of home, the negation of the enclosed and the snug. A microcosmic view of popular beliefs is afforded by the metamorphosis undergone by the poetic offering the Reverend E. H. Chapin published in *The Southern Literary Messenger* of September 1839. It was called "The Ocean-Buried," and began:

> "Bury me not in the deep deep sea!"
> The words came faint and mournfully,
> From the pallid lips of a youth, who lay
> On the cabin couch, where day by day
> He had wasted and pined.[11]

The lad asks rather to be laid in the churchyard on the green hillside by his father's grave, near the home, cot, and bower where he was raised so that his mother's prayers and his sister's tears can attend his rest. In the event, however, the unfortunate youth is lowered over the ship's side, "Where the billows bound and the wind sports free."

Within ten years the poem had acquired a printed musical score. Twenty years on it was not much heard in the parlors of America, but something called a "traditional cowboy song" was. It began:

> "Oh, bury me not on the lone prairie,"
> These words came low and mournfully
> From the pallid lips of a youth, who lay
> On his dying bed at the close of day.[12]

Unsurprisingly, this youth wants precisely the same green hillside grave as the luckless sailor and for exactly the same reasons. Alas, he had no better luck, and

In a narrow grave just six by three
We buried him there on the lone prairie

The graves depicted by Bryant and Cooper continued to dot the prairies of the imagination, a landscape so devoid of human meaning that words about the ocean could be applied to it also.

And then came the flood of indignation. At the time of the Midwest's great announcement of its self-discovery in the World's Columbian Exposition in 1893, a literary generation born on the prairies came into maturity and its theme was a double betrayal: the promise of the land betrayed by men—farmers, that is, betrayed by speculators; and the promise of men betrayed by the land—upright men coerced by labor to the stoop of beasts, and passionate women gone mad in shacks at the crossroad of the winds. Hamlin Garland, son of a westering Civil War veteran who homesteaded in Wisconsin, then Iowa, then South Dakota, only to go bust and backtrail to Wisconsin, sounded the keynote in *Main-Travelled Roads* (1891). The rudest stage of yeomanry had indeed succeeded the period of exploration, as earlier writers had predicted, but this was not followed by the New Englandy village of town green, trim houses, and bookish culture. Rather the home of toil was at one end of a road "hot and dusty in summer, and desolate and drear with mud in fall and spring," while in winter it was impassable, and at the other end was a town of shacks and tin.[13] The poor and weary predominated. Such culture as there was preached profit and the sinfulness of art.

The fantasized replication of Americanized European civilization had not occurred because between the emergence of the farmer and the growth of the market town, finance capital had intervened. Whatever their geographical proximity, the road from farm to town led through the metropolitan offices of banks, railroads, and land companies. Their lives were not in the control of the prairies' inhabitants. Their culture could neither grow coherently from their relationship to the land nor could the values of traditional culture—the best that man has thought and done—find a home in their midst. The latter culture was to be sought in the metropolis where social stratification and patronage American-style made it possible. In the amused dissection of

THE PRAIRIE STYLE OF FRANK LLOYD WRIGHT

Columbian Chicago found in the fiction of Henry Blake Fuller, artists and reformers go after Chicago with a will, but regardless of their projects—a painting or a settlement house—the paths they follow to accomplishment lead through the drawing rooms of Mrs. Eudoxia Pence.

The resulting prairie culture appeared mean, drab, and blighted to its native sons and daughters, and they sought the conscious life in Boston, New York, and Chicago, the mizzen, main, and fore masts of the American ship of culture. There, like Garland, they soon became deracinated and grafted themselves to a culture alien to their upbringing even as they bewailed the degradation of their home soil which made this necessary.

Some ten years after the Prairie style in architecture had been fully articulated, Carol Milford of Minneapolis married a doctor from Gopher Prairie, Minnesota, and made her home there. Anticipating her new life, Carol planned to bring beauty to a town which, however drab it then appeared, was bordered by lakes and flowed into a boundless prairie. But she seems never to have heard of the Prairie style, and the beautiful Gopher Prairie of her fantasy is Georgian. Her failure is a defeat at the hands of the powerfully corrosive culture of Gopher Prairie. But the narrative in which she lives is not called *Carol Kennicott* nor *Gopher Prairie,* but *Main Street.* The title is both a tip of Sinclair Lewis's hat to Hamlin Garland, who led the literary revolt from the prairie, and a reminder that a Gopher Prairie may be found wherever there is an American town big enough to have a Main Street.

The Prairie style has sometimes been regarded as a misnomer, a label that helps to distinguish a unique and consequential architectural achievement, but only a label, not an accurate description. The houses were, after all, designed in Chicago and not built on the real prairie. Such reservations have been countered by the contention that the coming-of-age of the Midwest, although dramatized by the rise of Chicago, was nevertheless regional and so should be identified in terms of the region's characteristic topography. Wright himself said, "We of the Middle West are living on the prairie. The prairie has a beauty of its own and we should recognize and accentuate this natural beauty, its quiet level."[14] Moreover, the effect of architectural space-in-motion not only blended inside and outside space but also captured a singularly potent feature of the prairies. Bryant in his poem, for example, had noted how still the prairies stood, only to add:

> Motionless?
> No—they are all unchained again. The clouds
> Sweep over with their shadows, and, beneath
> The surface rolls and fluctuates to the eye. (ll. 10–13)

The matter of greater significance is not whether the term Prairie style validly grows from other meanings of prairie, but whether that style once so named validly attached itself to the locale, made, as it were, the prairie its own. Of this there can be no doubt. Wright's Prairie style marked not only a major event in architectural history, it led to a major revision of cultural attitudes.

When we consider this revision in the context of the literary history of the prairie, we recognize that it is in good part a return to the outlook of the Romantic visionaries who had either little or no first-hand knowledge of the landscape. By Wright's day the real children of the prairie had lost the vision in pained reaction to the actuality. Also a native son, Wright transcended the actuality to embody what had only been vision for Bryant and Whitman.

Several years ago I took part in a symposium on the American Renaissance in art in connection with a show of paintings and artifacts from the period of 1878 to 1917. As now, my assignment then was to consider the literary context of the fine arts that formed the occasion. Then I was struck by how far in advance the writers were. The literary renaissance had preceded that in the fine arts by a quarter of a century; the painters were working in close cooperation with a patronage system which the writers of their day were exposing as the outgrowth of a social structure that denied the values that American literary artists had fought so hard to establish—denied what Whitman would have called American identity.

Now I am struck by quite the reverse. At a time when writers stood baffled and dismayed at the edge of the abyss which had opened between the promise of the prairies and the actuality of its culture and concluded that their literary task could only be a dismantling, a

THE PRAIRIE STYLE OF FRANK LLOYD WRIGHT

fellow artist, Frank Lloyd Wright, showed them the way to return to the dreamed-of ground and there to build.

NOTES

1. Sherman Paul, *Louis Sullivan: An Artist in American Thought* (New York: Prentice-Hall, 1962), 1.

2. Walt Whitman, "Song of Myself," *Leaves of Grass,* ed. Sculley Bradley and Harold W. Blodgett (New York: Norton, 1973), lines 12–13.

3. See, for example, Richard Bridgman, *The Colloquial Style in America* (New York: Oxford University Press, 1966).

4. Horatio Greenough, *The Travels, Observations, and Experiences of a Yankee Stonecutter* (Gainesville, Fla.: Scholars Facsimiles and Reprints, 1958), 33.

5. Ralph Waldo Emerson, *The Journals and Miscellaneous Notebooks,* 16 vols. (Cambridge, Mass.: Harvard University Press, 1961–82), 5:150.

6. William Dean Howells, *Literary Friends and Acquaintances* (Bloomington: Indiana University Press, 1968), 49.

7. William Cullen Bryant, "The Prairies," *The Literature of America,* 3 vols., ed. Irving Howe, Mark Schorer, and Larzer Ziff (New York: McGraw-Hill, 1971), 1:505, lines 1–4.

8. Henry Nash Smith, *Virgin Land* (Cambridge, Mass.: Harvard University Press, 1950), 220–24.

9. See, for example, two notable works of the 1920s: D. H. Lawrence, *Studies in Classic American Literature* (New York: Doubleday, 1951), and William Carlos Williams, *In the American Grain* (New York: New Directions, 1956).

10. Washington Irving, *A Tour on the Prairies* (London, 1835), 69.

11. Reverend E. H. Chapin, "The Ocean-Buried," *Southern Literary Messenger* 5, no. 9. (September 1839): 615–16.

12. "Bury Me Not on the Lone Prairie," *Songs of the Great American West,* ed. Irwin Silber (New York: Macmillan, 1967), 202.

13. Hamlin Garland, *Main-Travelled Roads* (New York: Signet, 1962), 12.

14. Quoted in Marcus Whiffen, *American Architecture Since 1780: A Guide to the Styles* (Cambridge, Mass.: MIT Press, 1969), 202.

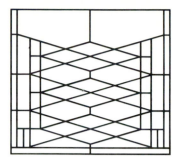

CONTRIBUTORS

Thomas H. Beeby is Dean of the School of Architecture at Yale University.

Carol R. Bolon is assistant professor in the departments of Art and South Asian Languages and Civilizations at the University of Chicago.

Joseph Connors is professor in the Department of Art History and Archaeology at Columbia University.

Donald Hoffmann is the art and architecture critic for *The Kansas City Star.*

Neil Levine is professor, and current chairman, in the Department of Fine Arts at Harvard University.

Julia Meech-Pekarik is an art historian living in New York City who specializes in Japanese art.

Robert S. Nelson is associate professor of art at the University of Chicago.

Vincent Scully is Sterling Professor of the History of Art at Yale University.

Linda Seidel is associate professor in the Department of Art and the Committee on General Studies in the Humanities at the University of Chicago.

David Van Zanten is professor of art history at Northwestern University.

Gwendolyn Wright is associate professor in The Graduate School of Architecture and Planning at Columbia University.

Larzer Ziff is the Caroline Donovan Professor of English Literature at The Johns Hopkins University.

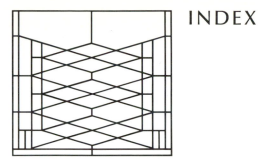

INDEX

Unity Temple, Oak Park, Illinois, xiii, xx, 47, 66

Utagawa Hiroshige, 126–27, 130, 131–32, 135, 137–38, 143, 145

Utamaro, 129

Van Gogh, Theo, 128

Van Gogh, Vincent, 128, 147–48

Van Vlieck, Edward Burr, 141

Venturi, Robert, xxi

Victoria Hotel, 7

Villa Stein, 13, 14

Villino Belvedere, Fiesole, Italy, 59–60

Viollet-le-duc, Eugene-Emanuel, 62, 94

Vitruvius, 85

Voysey, Charles F. Annesley, xix

W. Chandler house. *See* Chandler house

Wainwright Building, St. Louis, Missouri, 26–27, 76

Wainwright tomb, 7

Waller Apartments, 104

Ward Willitts house. *See* Willitts house

Wasmuth, Ernst, 21

Weir, J. Alden, 128, 139

Whistler, James Abbott McNeill, 10, 126–27

White, Charles E., Jr., 71–72, 93

Whitman, Walt, 86, 89–90, 91, 95, 173–76, 184

Wight, Peter B., 74

Wilde, Oscar, 125

Willitts, Ward, 131

Willitts house, xix

Williams house, Oak Park, 7–8, 15

Winslow, William, 9

Winslow house, River Forest, Illinois, 5–7, 8, 26–28, 30

Wolf house, xx

Wright, Catherine (FLW's first wife), 131

Wright houses and projects: 'Desert Dwelling' project, 40–42; Goethe Street, Chicago, project, 34; Oak Park house and studio, 23, 24–25, 26, 40, 61, 80, 81. *See also* Ocatilla; Taliesin; Taliesin West.

Wright, John Lloyd, 64, 68, 86

Wright, Olgivanna (FLW's third wife), xiii–xiv, 50

Yoshida Teruji, 141

Zola, Emile, 126

Zueblin, Charles, 105

12/95 17   10/60 25 (2000)